Policy Analysis

Policy Analysis

Jong Youl Lee

&

Chad Anderson

도서출판 대영문화사

Policy Analysis

Jong Youl Lee
(Professor, University of Incheon)

Chad Anderson
(Visiting Professor, University of Incheon)

Ilustration Jeoung Jae Hong

ISBN 978-89-7644 287-1
Published by Choon Hwan Lim
Daeyoung Moonhwasa Publishing Co.
178-2 Chungpa-dong 1ga Yongsan-gu Seoul 140-869, Korea

TEL (02) 716-3883, (02) 714-3062
FAX (02) 703-3839
Published on 25 August, 2008

Price ₩13,000

Preface

Policy analysis is a subject that is frequently taught at a graduate level. However, the reality of the Korean work environment dictates that universities do more to provide for the practical work-related skills that will help prepare for the student's first job. This is not intended as a scholarly book. It is a practical, student-oriented book designed for the undergraduate student, complete with pictures and examples drawn from the Korean experience students can relate to.

This book is designed to meet the specific needs of the Korean college student. First, it is in English. This is a global world. English has become the *de facto* international language of the world in the global era. This book will help Korean students become global leaders through learning and practicing practical English skills. Korea has had TOEIC fever for more than a decade now, and it shows no signs of dying down. However, behind the demand for TOIEC as a screening tool for employment lies the more fundamental demand for English communication skills. This book was written with an English-language course in mind. The language and content have been kept deliberately simple in order to give the Korean learner of policy analysis confidence in applying English-language skills. While there is nothing in this book that would be out of place in an American college course, the language has been arranged to be less of a dense and daunting challenge to the Korean college student.

The Korean college student will have had many years of English languagc instruction and yet will still generally lack the basic confidence to apply their broad base of knowledge. The authors hope that this text will contribute to the process of students taking English away from the realm of multiple choice tests and use it for their own purposes to increase their opportunities in life.

Secondly, this text provides a simplified overview of an important set of practical job skills. Whether the student decides to go on to a career in the Korean civil service, in the service of local government, in a public corporation, or abandons the public sector for the corporate sector, policy analysis is a good introduction to the reality of the work world and the kinds of practical skills that will be useful in many of the more popular jobs.

We have deliberately simplified this process so that it is not like a standard graduate text in the subject. Instead, we have prepared a broader introduction to the topic that should be useful to the student, regardless of their eventual career.

Even outside of the office, the skills taught in this text are applicable to real life. We can all benefit from a deeper analysis of our problems and from a more systematic approach to our decisions. The successful student of policy analysis can apply these skills to other areas of their life and see positive results.

This course can help you live a better life, be a better and more effective citizen, and prepare for the real world of work, whether in the corporate or public sector. Take this class seriously and you will reap serious benefits.

Finally, we wish to make some acknowledgements to some of the people who were critical to getting this book into print. While our many colleagues, family, and friends provided generous help, Dr. M. Sohel Iqbal made a critical contribution without which this book simply would not have been possible. He is not the only one, though. Jiyoung Ro provided invaluable support and assistance, particularly at a crucial time. Choon Hwan Lim, president of Daeyoung Moonhwasa Publishing Company, was kind enough to endure the process of publishing a book in a difficult foreign language and nonetheless producing an attractive result. They all have our deep thanks.

Jong Youl Lee

Chad Anderson

Incheon, August 2008

Contents

List of Boxes

List of Figures

List of Tables

WEEK 1 Introduction

Summary

Policy analysis is a way of deconstructing policy. In other words, it is about taking apart the components of policy to understand it better. Policy analysis uses methods from a variety of disciplines. It may involve the analysis of the policy process as a whole in addition to specific policies. Generally, policy analysis is taught as a more advanced graduate field of study and the move to teach it at the undergraduate level is a desire to meet students' needs for practical job skills. As a field of study, it evolved from political science to embrace multiple disciplines. Its practice has been influenced by the rational model. It takes place at diverse organizational levels.

Policy analysis is connected to organizational context as well as administrative and political feasibility. It involves a problem-solving approach for the purpose of reaching sound policy decisions.

It is an art as much as a science as it involves experience and judgment. It requires a framework for practical application.

Students may think of policy analysis as something nobody but politicians, government bureaucrats, and policy specialists need to care about. Everyone uses policy analysis techniques in their daily life. When we decide the course to take or choose where to eat dinner, we are thinking about the pros and the cons of the different choices. This is the essence of the policy analysis process.

Policy analysis is a systematic and organized means of evaluation. It is used to evaluate public policy alternatives. It may also be used to evaluate existing government programs. Policy analysis often includes quantitative analysis and evaluative tools.

Policy analysis is used throughout the policy process. It is especially important in the formulation of policies. It is also very important in evaluating programs after they are implemented. Policy analysis may help describe the scope of a public problem. With the issue of youth unemployment, for example, a first step would be to determine how many young people want jobs. Policy analysis is used by decision-makers to develop and judge alternatives. After decision-makers choose a general approach, policy analysis can be used to assess the feasibility of the choices. Policy analysis uses economic, administrative, political, and ethical criteria to choose from among the available choices. The same methods can be used to evaluate programs to determine effectiveness and to decide whether they have achieved their expected results.

1 What is Policy Analysis?

Analysis means deconstructing or taking something apart. It is breaking something down into its basic parts to understand it better. Policy analysis is the examination of the basic parts of public policy. It may also mean the policy process. Another way to look at policy analysis is that it is the study of why policies are chosen and what their results are. MacRae and Wilde call policy analysis "the use of reason and evidence to choose the best policy among a number of alternatives."

[Figure 1-1] A Car Broken Down into Its Component Parts

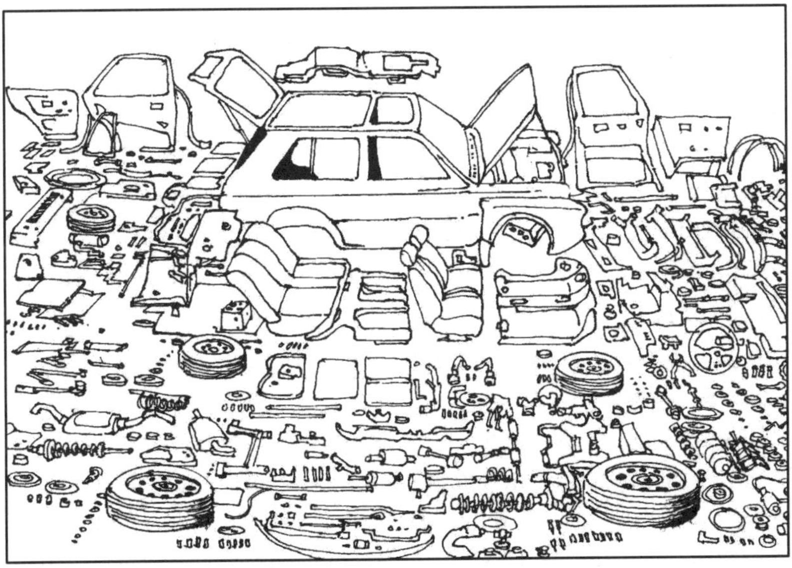

Policy analysis is the process of breaking down a thing into its component parts. Just as an auto mechanic must be able to tear apart a car and put it back together, so the policy analyst must be able to break down complicated public issues and analyze them in detail.

What is policy analysis? For basic purposes, policy analysis is a systematic way of thinking about practical problems. The characteristics of the analyst and decision-makers are not important. The product of the analysis is central. The quality of analysis is particularly important along three dimensions. These dimensions are system, practicality, and communication. If all three are not in place or are not well-balanced, policy analysis will not support practical action.

System is important for three reasons. All are related to the nature of organizational systems. The first is because policy analysis is grounded in a particular political/administrative system. The Korean policy analyst must deal with a different system from the one an American analyst must address. Someone in the national government deals with a different system from an analyst in the Seoul City government. The second reason is that policy issues and problems arise and are resolved within the context of complicated social systems. It is important for analysts to understand the interactions of organizations and their environment. The final reason is that policies and programs themselves can be seen as systems. They exist in and interact with their environment. They have various inputs that they transform into outputs in a process that repeats itself.

Practicality is a necessary dimension of policy analysis because the subject addresses practical problems. Theory is important and useful for understanding problems, as well as for developing an understanding of causal relationships. However, the most elaborate and rigorous theory will not solve problems. Practicality, the attention to what works in a given situation, is paramount here. This is one reason why professional analysis and political analysis play such a big role in the policy process.

Communication is the life-blood of policy. Policy analysts need timely and accurate information. The public and decision makers need to communicate their preferences. Feedback in the form of criticism is necessary for functional implementation of any policy or program. Policy targets and clients need to provide feedback. Stakeholders need to provide their feedback. Literally, none of the stages of policy analysis are possible without multiple clear streams of communication.

Policy analysis uses many different methods. It is multidisciplinary and uses a variety of subjects to obtain information. This is necessary for assessing problems and thinking clearly about alternative ways to resolve them. The information gathered in a policy analysis also shapes the public debate and influences the decision-making process over what constructive actions to take. Policy analysis encourages critical thinking. Deep and deliberate thinking is necessary to ascertain the causes of public problems. It may also determine the various ways policy actors might respond to public problems and help decide which policy choices make the most sense.

Policy analysis may also mean examining the parts of the policymaking process. These may include policy formulation and implementation, in addition to substantive public policy issues. The collection and interpretation of information is crucial to clarify the causes and effects of public problems, as well as to estimate the likely results of the different policy options.

The aspect of analysis that makes students think it is just for specialists is that it is a quasi-scientific process. Analysis often uses scientific knowledge in the political process and frequently employs scientific methods. These scientific processes may be both empirical (descriptive) and normative (value-oriented).

This means that scientific methods may be used empirically to describe problems. They may also be used normatively to apply values in particular situations.

2 Policy Analysis and Public Administration

Policy analysis plays a key role in public administration. At the current time, the discipline of policy analysis provides a set of tools that are essential for the mission of public administration. As a practical hands-on field of study, public administration needs practical tools to carry out its missions. Policy analysis is one of those tools.

Public policy analysis draws on multiple disciplines and perspectives. As a practice, its analysis may rest on the methods and tools of economics, political science, operations research, history, sociology, and even psychology. It deals with substantive issues across a wide realm. This type of multidisciplinary analysis and reporting requires a certain level of skill and experience. This probably explains why courses in policy analysis tend to appear more often in graduate public administration programs than in undergraduate programs.

Policy analysis and public policy as fields of study explicitly rejected public administration. The founders of the new programs gave reasons for this decision. They thought public administration was descriptive rather than prescriptive. They thought it was preoccupied by institutions rather than by choices or actions. They were restricted to the single discipline of political science and thus lacked interdisciplinary vision. However, the reasons were political as well as intellectual.

Ironically, as public policy curricula have evolved, they have increasingly included institutional analysis. Similarly, policy evaluation and policy analysis have become increasingly important in the practice of public administration. In part, this reflects the importance of the administrative rationality paradigm of organization. The movement to rationalize policy making using techniques drawn from various disciplines follows logically from the rationality paradigm. The study of the process of policy making comes from the same source. Although the rational model is not universally embraced, it surely describes what many public managers do, attempt to do, or believe they are supposed to do. Analysis is a major activity in government at all levels. The literature on the uses and effects of policy analysis in government agencies, the Blue House, the National Assembly, and local government is abundant. Personal computing, the internet, and analytic training have created a huge potential for personnel at lower levels to perform analysis that used to be the domain of specialists. Moreover, as local autonomy has increased responsibility for various policy areas, the need for local-level policy analysis is growing. With the growing emphases on service delivery, productivity, competition between public and private providers, and on quality management, the need for analysis in public organizations will surely increase.

A course in public policy analysis can serve as a natural culmination for an undergraduate program in public administration. It pulls together and integrates everything the student has studied before.

3 Policy Analysts and Public Administrators

Once organizational structures for programs have been created, public administrators turn their attention to the routine decisions concerning personnel, budgets, and operating procedures that help determine how well programs will meet their goals.

Policy analysts consider questions of organizational design and administrative feasibility. They try to influence the choice of programs through the political process. A public administrator focuses exclusively on doing a good job of executing the policies that have been chosen. A policy analyst also considers the choice of what is to be done. Public administration has gradually come to include policy analysis among its professional activities. One reason is that large bureaus and vague legislative mandates associated with an expanded public role in society require administrators to choose among alternative policies. In this way they actually become consumers and producers of the policy analysis relevant to their agencies.

The "new" public administration explicitly abandons the notion that administration should be separate from politics. Its practitioners seek to influence the adoption as well as implementation of policies. Professional training, therefore, must also include methods for effectively participating in the political process as well as for predicting the consequences of alternative policies so that informed choices can be made. Training in public administration thus often includes coursework in policy analysis, even though its primary focus remains management and operational decision making.

A relatively recent formulation of public administration has been called public management. It has been framed by the study of governance, regimes of laws, rules, judicial decisions, and administrative practices that constrain, prescribe, and enable the provision of publicly supported goods and services. Although this broader perspective encompasses managerial practices, it explicitly deals with the choice of organizational forms, a decision appropriately informed by policy analysis.

4 Purposes of Policy Analysis

Policy analysis involves a problem solving approach. It also includes the collection and interpretation of information, as well as some attempt to predict the consequences of alternative courses of action.

The fundamental purpose of policy analysis is to make it easier to reach sound policy decision. As a result, policy analysis may include the examination of problems and issues, as well as of legislation or proposed legislation, the position of political leadership, agency programs, private sector organizations and their policies, and any other subject of significance which calls for attention and decision-making.

Policy analysis requires the analysis of underlying assumptions and their implications. Analysts must investigate information gaps and internal inconsistencies. They need to be aware of conflicts within their goals, policies, and programs. Political consequences are important. Impacts on society, the economy, and the environment need to be forecast. The problems of administrative implementation need to be projected and accounted for. Institutional aspects must be observed. Problems of coordinating interdisciplinary impact must be negotiated. The hypothetical alternatives need to be listed, along with disqualifying reasons for those ruled out. The realistic alternatives must be presented with their pros and cons. Finally, policy analysis must include all of the evaluation, oversight, and follow-up requirements and procedures.

Even though this seems like a long and exhaustive list, a failure to include any step may break the policy chain and result in failure of the entire program due to a single fault in one part.

5 Basic Preparation for Policy Analysis

Although policy analysis is presented as scientific, it is as much an art and a craft as a science. The successful policy analyst is an artist of sorts who manages to apply the basic skills of the discipline within a realistic perspective of the role of government in society that is at least internally consistent.

Preparation in five areas is essential for the purpose of achieving this successful application:

- Gathering, organizing, and communicating information appropriate to the policy situation
- A perspective for contextualizing social problems
- Technical policy analysis skills
- An understanding of politics and organizational behavior
- An ethical framework

Gathering, Organizing, and Communicating Information Appropriate to the Policy Situation

Analysts must know how to gather, organize, and communicate information, particularly in situations with strict deadlines or where access to the relevant people is limited. They must be able to develop strategies for quickly understanding the nature of policy problems. These strategies should be able to accommodate consideration of a broad range of possible solutions. They must also be able to identify, at least qualitatively, the likely costs and benefits of the alternatives. Having done so, they need to communicate these assessments to decision makers.

A Perspective for Contextualizing Social Problems

Analysts need a perspective for putting perceived social problems in context. They need to be able to answer questions like "When is it legitimate for government to intervene in private affairs?" The normative answer to this question has usually been based on the concept of market failure. This is where the pursuit of private interest does not lead to an efficient use of societal resources or a fair distribution of societal goods (See Box 1-1). The analyst needs a perspective that includes government failure as well as market failure.

Technical Policy Analysis Skills

Analysts need technical skills that help them to predict the consequences of alternative policies. Economics and statistics serve as primary sources for these skills. If you want a career in policy analysis, you would be advised to take courses in these subjects.

An Understanding of Politics and Organizational Behavior

Analysts must have an understanding of politics and organizational

[Box 1-1] *High Fuel Prices: Market Failure for Truck Drivers?*

Environmental problems like pollution are often cited as examples of market failure. What about labor problems? Different nations regulate their labor markets to different extents.

The rapid rise in gasoline prices has hit truck drivers in Korea especially hard. *Hankyoreh* reported on May 27, 2008 that many truck drivers would be forced out of work unless employers increased their freight rates. They reported on the example of a trip from Changwon, South Gyeongsang to Seoul that paid about ₩600,000 for a two-day trip. The price of the diesel fuel needed for the trip was about ₩490,000, in addition to a ₩50,000 toll and ₩30,000 for food. This does not count the costs of insurance and maintenance. The basic problem was that oil prices doubled to about ₩2,000 per liter from ₩1,100 in a year, while the freight rates stayed almost the same.

The Korean Transport Workers' Union stopped working for eight days through May 26. A union representative was quoted as saying, "If the government doesn't take special measures (to address the fuel price problem), there is nothing we can do but to stop driving. Such a situation will cause a serious logistics crisis and enormous social conflicts." The union also urged the government to better regulate oil refiners, strengthen public transport routes and implement price controls on transport fares as promised.

Discussion Questions

- The market has not met the needs of these workers, but has it failed enough to justify government action?
- Is this a problem that truck drivers and logistics companies can solve or does the government need to take action?
- Find out how the government addressed this situation. Do you agree with their solution?

– Hankyoreh Media Company

behavior in order to predict the feasibility of the adoption and successful implementation of specific policies. This knowledge will perhaps also allow them to influence the process. Understanding the world views of decision makers and potential opponents helps the analyst marshal evidence and prepare arguments more effectively.

An Ethical Framework

Analysts should have an ethical framework that explicitly takes account of their relationships to decision makers. Analysts often face dilemmas when their perceptions of the public interest diverge substantially from the private preferences and interests of decision makers.

6 A Framework for Policy Analysis

What does the analyst do when they must face a complicated policy issue? Suppose you are a new policy analyst for the Seoul City Council. Your first project is to investigate and evaluate alternative pollution control measures for the Han River. The problem has so many possible impacts you wonder how you will ever sort them out. You even wonder where to begin. You can always try to concentrate and work really hard, hoping you will eventually develop a feel for the situation. This approach amounts to little more than trial-and-error. You might get lucky and stumble across a good policy. You are more likely to get a headache trying to achieve little. It would be better to have a standard procedure that would at least help you get started working on this complex policy issue.

Policy analysts have experimented with a variety of ways to structure complex problems like this one. Edith Stokey and Richard Zeckhauser suggest the following five-part framework as a starting point. As you gain experience in thinking about policy choices analytically, you may wish to revise it to suit your own style. This is just a guide to help the inexperienced get started and not a set of rules to be followed no matter what.

Establishing the Contcxt

What is the underlying problem that must be dealt with? What specific objectives are to be pursued in confronting this problem?

Laying Out the Alternatives

What are the alternative courses of action? What are the possibilities for gathering further information?

Predicting the Consequences

What are the consequences of each of the alternative actions? What techniques are relevant for predicting these consequences? If outcomes are uncertain, what is the estimated likelihood of each?

Valuing the Outcomes

By what criteria should we measure success in pursuing each objective? Recognizing that some alternatives will inevitably be superior with respect to others, how should different combinations of valued objectives be compared with one another?

Making a Choice

Considering all aspects of the analysis, what is the preferred course of action?

Stokey and Zeckhauser do not mean to imply that an analyst will always proceed in an orderly fashion from one stage of the analysis to the next. Reality rarely operates so neatly. The main point is that each of these five critical areas must be dealt with. The conduct of an analysis will usually turn out in practice to be an iterative process. This means that the analyst will work back and forth among the tasks of identifying problems, defining objectives, enumerating possible alternatives, predicting outcomes, establishing criteria, and valuing tradeoffs, to refine the analysis.

This is a common-sense approach. It is easier to keep track of where you are in this process (to avoid going over the same ground again and again) if you keep in the mind a basic framework. Then you can relate every aspect of the analysis to a step in the process and keep it all organized. Furthermore, decision makers using your analysis will thank you for strict adherence to a clearly visible structure that makes the analysis easier to read and to understand. A systematic approach should open the analysis up for evaluation and debate.

Discussion Questions

1. What is policy analysis?
2. How is policy analysis a useful subject for career development?
3. Should policy analysis be connected to politics, or should it be neutral?
4. What are the purposes of policy analysis?
5. What is necessary for successful policy analysis?
6. How can a framework help with policy analysis?

Vocabulary

systematic	rationality
system	professional training
practicality	public management
communication	artist
multidisciplinary	market failure
empirical	government failure
normative	context

References

Bovbjerg, Randall R. (1985). "What Is Policy Analysis?." *Journal of Policy Analysis and Management,* 5 (1), Autumn: 154-158.

Carver, Robert H. (1996). Where Does Policy Analysis Belong in the Undergraduate Public Administration Major?. *PS: Political Science and Politics,* 29 (3), Sept.: 521-525.

"High Oil Prices Forcing Truck Drivers out of Business." http://english.hani.co.kr/arti/english_edition/e_national/289886.html

Kraft, E. Michael, and Furlong, R. Scott (2004). *Public Policy: Politics, Analysis, and Alternatives.* CQ Press: Washington, DC.

MacRae, Duncan, Wilde, James A. (1979). *Policy Analysis for Public Decisions.* Druxbury, North Scituate, MA.

Stokey, Edith, and Zeckhauser, Richard (1978). *A Primer for Policy Analysis.* W.W. Norton & Company: New York, NY.

Weimer, L. David, and Vining, R. Aidan (2005). *Policy Analysis: Concepts and Practice.* Pearson Prentice Hall: Englewood Cliffs, NJ.

WEEK 2 The Nature of Policy Analysis

Summary
Policy analysis usually involves comparing policy options. It is complicated and rarely easy. It is both a technical and a political process.
Policy analysis is a broad field and its practice may involve a wide variety of different choices about how and where to place emphasis. These include choices as to the level of pragmatism and practicality, policy relevance, faithfulness to mainstream values, and democracy.
Policy analysis has six distinguishing characteristics. They are the field's broad concerns, its quantitative aspect, a focus on implementation, a normative orientation, the use of hard science, and program experimentation.

Policy analysis usually means the judgment of the relative value of policy alternatives. It is a process of assessment. It is the systematic investigation of alternative policy options. It is also the assembly and integration of the evidence for and against each option. Policy analysis is not intended to make policy decisions but to inform the process of public deliberation and debate. It does not substitute for the debate, but supplies the tools that enable the debate.

[Figure 2-1] Policy Analysis is a Systematic Process

Policy analysis is a process of assessment that systematically investigates alternative policy options. Policy analysis also assembles and integrates evidence for and against each option to inform the process of public deliberation and debate.

The study of public policy and the conduct of policy analysis are not simple. Public problems are usually complex and multi-faceted. That means that they have many sides and are difficult to decide. People frequently disagree over how serious problems are, what can be done about them, and the respective role of government and the private sector in addressing them. Some problems, such as global climate change or the challenge of balancing all of the demands placed on the economy, are huge.

It is hard even to know where to start. With some problems it may be easier to evaluate and conceptualize the issue. However, no public problem is simple. If you think a public controversy is simple, then you are probably not considering an important factor in your analysis. If public issues were simple, there would be no controversy and no debate and therefore no need for policy analysis. Unfortunately, most problems are not easy and require policy analysis to break them down to a comprehensible level.

One of the primary functions of policy analysis is to provide necessary information. Another important function is to provide decision makers with thoughtful and impartial assessments during the policy process. The information may not be widely available, or citizens and policy makers may not be able to understand it well enough. This is particularly true when decisions must be made quickly because of deadlines or when the issues are politically controversial.

Under these conditions, policy analysis has the power to clarify issues, provide available alternatives, and forecast the effects of decisions that citizens and policy makers might choose. Policy analysis involves anticipating the consequences of decisions and thinking seriously and critically about them. It is an alternative to making decisions based on ideology or minimal analysis.

The solution to any controversial public problem is rarely achieved by relying solely on government officials, policy analysts, or other experts. Everyone always has a different judgment and this is reflected in what they think represents the "best" choice. Political choices involve potential conflict because they inevitably involve questions about the likely effectiveness, costs, winners, and losers of potential policies. The question of whether an action can be justified on ethical or moral grounds is another major source of dispute. The nature of policy analysis is shaped by the political context in which it occurs.

The existence of politics is obvious in areas of public controversy like the controversy over the import of American beef, choosing the location of a nuclear waste dump, or the design of a new educational reform. Issues like these address values in an obvious and fundamental way. Policy choices like these are based on political preferences as well as impartial assessment of the problem and possible solutions. Policy analysis can determine the nature of the problem. It may also put forth the policy choices. Finally the process evaluates each choice using the various different standards that are selected as evaluative criteria.

[Figure 2-2] Solving a Problem is like Solving a Puzzle

Policy analysts work together to try to assemble the best information available to find effective, efficient, and equitable solutions to public problems.

When you hear political and policy discussion in informal public settings, the level of the discussion is informal and tends toward simplistic statements about whatever issue is being discussed. Citizens frequently air their views of government and public issues in this way, but they rarely think systematically about the cause of problems. Nor do they think of what kind of policy action is most appropriate, given all of the realistic political and governmental limitations. Policy analysts hope to raise the level of such discussions, even if it remains unlikely that conversations on the subway will be anchored in sophisticated data analysis.

7 Kinds of Policy Analysis

There is never a single correct way to conduct a policy study or one set of methods or tools to use. This does not depend on the field of inquiry. Analysts face important choices about the kind of assessment needed for a given study and what approaches to use.

Basic Causes versus Practical Solutions

One of the basic questions that all analysts must answer is whether they should focus on the root causes of public problems or examine policy actions that might relieve the symptoms of a pressing problem but do nothing about its underlying causes. If we take the example of a complex problem like crime, which is the subject of an entire field of study, it might not even be possible to address the underlying causes. The science of criminology has determined than men commit more crimes than women. Does this mean that all men should be locked up as potential criminals? Young men commit more crime than older men. Maybe men should be monitored until old age? While the facts regarding root causes may not be in doubt, their practical implications are limited.

Instead, government policy involves a complicated mix of punishment and rehabilitation that is designed to deter crime and reduce its incidence when it does happen. In this case the approach tends towards the practical and tries to minimize effects instead of eliminate crime all together. In other cases, it may be more effective to address root causes to put an end to an issue once and for all.

Comprehensive versus Policy-Specific

There is always a question of how comprehensive and rigorous analysis should be to ensure the credibility of results. The more credible and comprehensive a study is the longer and more costly it is. A less comprehensive and less rigorous study might provide pertinent results faster and cheaper, but it may reduce the credibility of the results. The direction an analysis goes depends on the nature of the problem, as well as on the nature and position of the analyst.

The most complex, controversial, and costly policy choices might require the most comprehensive analysis, while more limited studies might suffice in other situations. Academic scientists favor rigorous and comprehensive studies, regardless of whether they come from the "hard" sciences or the social sciences. They place a high value on scientific and methodological precision because they believe that only scientific investigations produce knowledge that inspires confidence. On the other hand, a study can take so long to complete that it has less impact on policy decisions than it might have had if the results were known earlier. There is more than one case where the government has already acted by the time a study is released. Scientists follow the timetable that their process requires, whereas government action follows a more political logic and often needs to appear within a certain political cycle in order to be considered effective.

Following versus Challenging Social Norms

Analysts must decide whether to follow public values and adhere closely to social norms and mainstream public values. An alternative would be to challenge approaches and values that may not work anymore and propose new values or new ways of thinking about a problem. Martin Rein advocated making the analyst a moral critic who questions the value and belief assumptions of policy research. Rein identified three approaches to policy problems, ranging from the most mainstream to the most critical. The first approach is to use consensual or mainstream approaches. The second approach is to use contentious or value critical approaches. Finally, the third (and most radical) approach is to use fundamental paradigm-challenging approaches. Most policy analysis uses the first approach, a smaller number of studies use the second approach, while an insignificant number of studies use paradigmshifting approaches. Even so, these studies have their place as many public problems could use bold thinking and might benefit from a new perspective, or at least from a radical challenge.

Rational Analysis versus Politics

Policy analysts are trained to engage in rational assessment of public problems and solutions. As such, they often use economic analysis and other quantitative methods to find the most logical and efficient ways to deal effectively with public problems. However, our nation has a democratic system. What is the responsibility of the analyst to get the citizen involved for the purpose of increasing public participation? There is an inherent tension between the rational scientific decision-making process and the political process, which is often ruled by limited information and popular values rather than by exacting information. The decision to approve the KORUS FTA involved technical economic factors, but the public reaction to it was based on their perception of how well it served their interests (see Box 2-1).

[Box 2-1] *FTA or No FTA?*

The consideration of the Korean-USA Free Trade Agreement (KORUS FTA) was seen through starkly different lenses, depending on where people stand on the political spectrum and in relation to government. People in government and on the right of the political spectrum tended to focus on the technical details of the agreement, while those in the center and on the left who were outside of government tended to see the agreement in more philosophical terms. *Chosun Ilbo* reported extensively on the subject. The paper reported on September 8, 2006 that the two sides were exchanging concessions. Korea's chief negotiator Kim Jonghoon told reporters, "The US accepted our position that their textile tariff concessions were highly disappointing," and, "The overall negotiations are going on smoothly... There are signs that the US is becoming gradually positive in the negotiations." The US asked Korea to raise the ceiling on foreign equity ownership of cable networks from 49% to 51% and the two parties agreed that US asset management firms could operate funds created by Korean financial institutions, while the US remained reluctant to ease anti-dumping restrictions, one of Korea's top priorities (dumping is the practice of selling at a lower price overseas than domestically, a strategy that had cost many US jobs).

In stark contrast, *Chosun Ilbo* highlighted the Korean Alliance Against KORUS FTA's national report, which opposed the agreement with the US. It featured statements like, "A Korea-US free trade agreement is effectively an accord to surrender our sovereignty," and "The Korean Peninsula would face a military threat from the FTA since there would be repercussions from China and North Korea." The paper also reported on Korean participation at an American Labor Day rally against the free trade pact march under a banner that read "We Want the Rights to Health, Education and Public Services" (*sic*). Clearly, the concerns of both groups were very different, those opposed to the agreement raising more fundamental concerns about the nature of the relationship between Korea and the US. They were also more likely to question the working of the market in Korea.

Discussion Questions

- How important are trade agreements between nations?
- What difference does the relative size of the nations make (the larger US and smaller Korea or the larger Korea and

the smaller Chile)?
- On what basis should trade agreements be decided? Should they be judged on the merit of the substance of the agreement? Is it okay to dismiss them entirely on ideological grounds?
- Would you support such agreements more if you felt that you, personally, would benefit?

– Chosun Ilbo

8 Characteristics of Policy Analysis as a Discipline

Six characteristics set policy analysis apart from other related disciplines and professions.

First, policy analysis is concerned with broad policy issues and interdisciplinary aspects when compared with economics or operations research. The political and administrative factors involved in decisions are good examples. A decision may be economically sound, but administratively complicated or politically impossible.

Second, policy analysis is more quantitative, statistical, and mathematical than political science or public administration. From the standpoint of analysts as well as practitioners, the collection, analysis, and testing of large data sets dominates the analyst's job whether the data comes from a study of the efficiency of local garbage collection or from official central government databases.

Third, policy analysis is more concerned with the implementation and management of policy when compared to systems analysis or operations research. Any analysis is not complete if it does not give specific attention to how policy choices may fail during implementation.

Fourth, policy analysis is more normative than economics. While it does address descriptive issues, it is also concerned with issues like liberty, equity, and with ethical dilemmas.

Fifth, policy analysis and public management is often involves technology, engineering, and physical science. For example, the job of analyzing the various options in building the KTX required understanding the complex technologies involved.

Finally, policy analysis is closely associated with programmatic experimentation. This means that analysts try new approaches and use the data gathered during implementation to design future approaches.

Discussion Questions

1. What are the purposes of policy analysis?
2. What kind of analysis would you prefer?
3. When is it necessary to understand root causes?
4. What makes policy analysis different from other disciplines?
5. How pragmatic should analysis be?
6. How much should analysis challenge mainstream opinion?
7. What is the responsibility of analysis to democracy?

Vocabulary

assessment
public deliberation
public controversy
root causes
consensual
contentious
paradigm-shifting
rational assessment
interdisciplinary
normative
experimentation
systematic investigation

References

Bovbjerg, Randall R. (1985). "What Is Policy Analysis?." *Journal of Policy Analysis and Management*, 5 (1), Autumn: 154-158.

deLeon, Peter (1997). *Democracy and the Policy Sciences.* State University of New York Press: Albany, NY.

"Fighting the Future with the Rhetoric of Yesteryear" http://english.chosun.com/w21data/html/news/200607/200607310036.html

"Korea, U.S. Compromise on Farm Goods, Textiles" http://english.chosun.com/w21data/html/news/200609/200609080023.html

Kraft, E. Michael, and Furlong, R. Scott (2004). *Public Policy: Politics, Analysis, and Alternatives*. CQ Press: Washington DC.

Rein, Martin (1976). *Social Science and Public Policy.* Penguin Books: New York, NY.

Weimer, L. David, and Vining, R. Aidan (2005). *Policy Analysis: Concepts and Practice*. Pearson Prentice Hall: Englewood, Cliffs, NJ.

Wilson, James Q. (1977). *Thinking about Crime.* Vintage Books: New York, NY.

WEEK 3 The Process of Policy Analysis

Summary

Policy analysis involves five information components and six analytical methods. The policy analyst must gather and judge the value and relevance of information.

There are three broad types of analysis.

Scientific analysis follows rigorous procedures in the pursuit of fundamental scientific truth. Scientific analysis tries to improve the capacity of decision makers to make informed judgments. Professional analysis tries to provide an informed range of alternatives.

Political analysis supports and argues in favor of specific, often ideological alternatives.

Policy analysis is divided into five steps. The first step is defining and analyzing the problem, followed by constructing alternatives. Next is developing evaluative criteria and then assessing the alternatives. The final step is drawing conclusions.

Policy analysis is a process of inquiry involving five components related to one another through six policy-analysis methods, as illustrated by the framework presented in Figure 3-1 (See also Week 5 for Types of Policy Information).

Policy problems give rise to policy alternatives, some of which become policy actions, leading to policy outcomes that are the basis of policy performance. Forecasting gives alternatives. Recommendation changes alternatives into actions that are monitored for their outcomes. Policy outcomes lead to problem structuring and new definitions of policy problems. Evaluation of outcomes defines performance and leads to new alternatives. Performance gives practical interference that affects policy problems.

[Figure 3-1] The Process of Policy Analysis

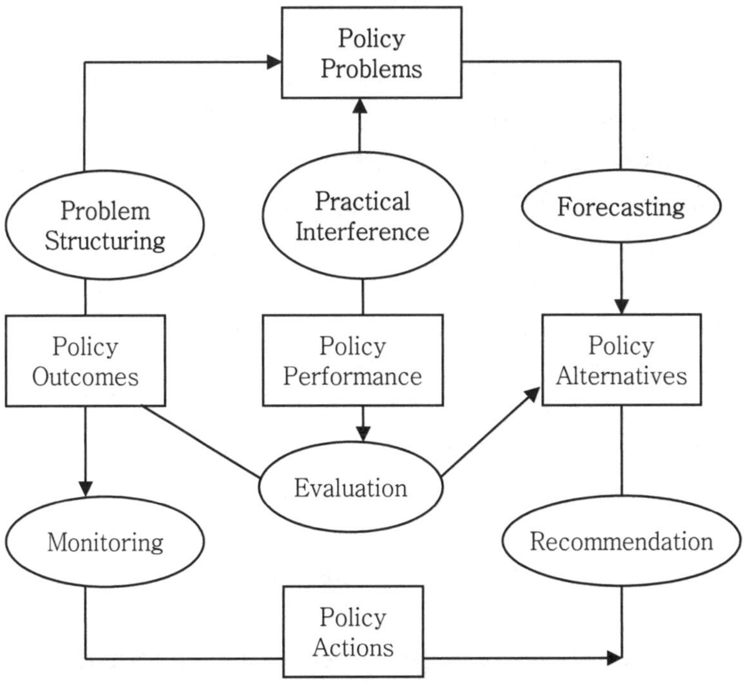

9 Types of Policy Analysis

The number of policy studies is determined in part by the number of policy-oriented research institutes, or so-called think tanks. The number of interest groups that participate in the policy process and try to affect it by shaping popular and elite opinion also contribute to policy analysis. Environmental activists, corporate trade associations, professional organizations, and unions all have a stake in policy decisions made by government. Most of them watch legislation and agency decisions that may affect their areas of concern.

Organizations that do policy analysis are numerous due to the nature of government institutions and the political process. Divided government authority, where more than one agency or bureau theoretically has jurisdiction over a problem creates many opportunities. As a result, interest group lobbying and policy analysis are often conducted outside of government. The weakening of political parties and their non-ideological orientation strengthens the opportunities for determined interest groups and ideological think tanks.

The great amount of information now easily available to the public and policy makers, as well as the number of people doing policy analysis means that information overload is increasingly a problem. Decision makers try to deal with all of the many reports and studies available on the average public policy topic. The ability to do quality policy analysis can help address the problem. Those who can determine the important and the meaningless information will be sought after for their analytical skills.

This kind of policy analyst gathers critical information in a timely way, analyzes it, and makes wise judgments on the basis of the best information available. There are different kinds of analysis. Decision makers, including the public; need to be able to tell the difference between useful analysis and information that is slanted or misleading.

Policy analysis may belong to one of three general categories. These are political, professional, and scientific. All have a place and are legitimate, but they may have very different goals and objectives. They also tend to use different methods and standards. Table 3-1 reviews the distinctions between the three types.

[Table 3-1] Types of Policy Analysis

Type of Analysis	Objectives	Approaches	Limitations
Scientific	· Search for 'truth' and build theory about policy actions and effects	· Use the scientific method to test hypotheses and theories · Aim for objective and rigorous analysis · Policy relevance less important than advancing knowledge	· May be too theoretical · May not adequately address information needs of decision makers
Professional	· Analyze policy alternatives for solving public problems	· Synthesize research and theory to understand consequences of policy alternatives · Evaluate current programs and their effects	· Research and analysis may be too narrow due to time and resource constraints · May neglect fundamental causes of public problems

		· Aim for objectivity, but with goal of applicability to policy debate	
Political	· Advocate and support preferred policies	· Use legal, economic, and political arguments consistent with value positions · Level of objectivity and rigor varies · Aim to influence policy debate to realize organizational goals and values	· Often ideological or partisan · May not be credible · May lack analytic depth

Scientific studies search for objective fact and truth. They try to construct and verify theories about policy actions and effects. They use the scientific method and employ rigorous analytical techniques. They are not usually intended to influence policy directly and may be too theoretical to be of practical use for decision makers in a given case.

Social science studies in the scientific category are not usually intended to influence public policy directly. Their purpose is to increase the policy maker's capacity for judgment. As a result, scientists frequently fail to provide specific answers in specific situations. In contrast, work that falls into the professional category, such as policy analysis from think tanks, is nearly always directed at policy makers with the clear intent of providing answers to policy questions.

Professional analysis looks at policy alternatives for solving public problems. It is less rigorous than scientific inquiry. It lacks the strict universal standards of science. Even so, it tries to be objective while combining theory with more practical research. This is for the purpose of addressing issues that are more practical in the policy debate. This sort of analysis may lack the thoroughness of scientific research and may miss some important causes, focusing on some at the expense of others.

The political variety of analysis is the level that is designed specifically for the policy debate. It consists of a variety of arguments drawn from relevant disciplines that present a case to influence decision makers. Political analysis is designed to be consistent with certain political values. This analysis is often focused on advancing specific solutions. It may be ideological. The quality varies widely. Its partisan nature means that it may be less credible as facts are more often chosen to advance a specific case.

Some think tanks should be placed in the political category because they have explicit ideological missions. For example, the Heritage Foundation in the US explicitly tries to advocate conservative and market-oriented solutions. While it calls itself a research institution, it is unlike more neutral think tanks like the government-run Korea Development Institute, which suggests a range of solutions not connected to a specific partisan viewpoint.

[Box 3-1] *Government Intervention on Beef Policy*

The story of President Lee's change in the standards for importing beef from the United States should be familiar to all Koreans. President Lee offered to resume import of American beef in order to encourage the American Congress to approve the KORUS FTA that Democrats held up because of restrictions on beef and an imbalance in automobile imports. He chose the opportunity of the world food animal organization OIE upgrading the US's Bovine Spongiform Encephalopathy (BSE) status to controlled risk (a higher standard than Korea met at the time) to improve the standards that Korea had for the import of meat from other countries in the same class.

The government saw the objectives of this intervention in terms of getting the KORUS FTA passed. However, the negative public perception of Lee following repeated scandals over appointees and an increasing sense that he was out of touch with the public meant that he became the issue.

While protesters often cited food safety concerns, the government and protesters were not talking about the same concerns. The government offered to resign and tried to resolve minimal safety issues, renegotiating beef standards to match those of other nations that import US beef, while Koreans abroad and in the US had no concerns over American beef. Even as the government tried to resolve the issue, the KCTU pledged to block imports of US beef. There remained a lack of agreement and shared understanding of the issues surrounding the import of American beef. While conservatives focused on the objectives of the original intervention, protesters and many in the larger public only paid attention to the original issue as a symbol of larger problems with the Lee administration.

Discussion Questions

- What should be the policy for importing American beef?
- Would it be okay to ban American beef? Is it okay even if it means that Korea would have stricter standards for American beef than it does for other countries with the same

OIE rating?

- President Lee's intervention was designed to help pass the KORUS FTA negotiated under President Noh. How could he have achieved that goal without raising massive protests?

- Hankyoreh Media Company, *Chosun Ilbo*

10 The Steps of Policy Analysis

The word analysis comes from Greek roots and means to break down into component parts. Teachers of policy analysis usually explain the analytical process as a series of steps. The most common approach to policy analysis is to think of it as a series of stages, which are the elements of rational problem solving. According to rational decision making, a problem is defined, the goals and objectives are decided, a range of alternative solutions are considered, and each of the alternatives is evaluated to clarify their consequences. Finally, the alternative with the greatest potential for solving the problem is recommended or chosen. This process is similar to the way most people make everyday decisions, even if people do it much more casually than in the formal rational decision process.

The discussion below summarizes the major steps in policy analysis and the kinds of questions analysts ask. It also shows how each stage of analysis might apply to a particular policy problem, in this case car accidents caused by cell phones.

Each step is considered briefly here as a summary description of what policy analysis aspires to do.

[Figure 3-2] A Driver Using a Cell Phone

Many car accidents are caused by driver distractions like cell phones, the radio, drinking coffee, and applying make up.

Define and Analyze the Problem

Defining the problem is the first step of policy analysis. The general meaning and the policy analysis term of problem are different. For policy analysts a problem specifically refers to the existence of an unsatisfactory situation (or set of conditions) for which relief is sought. This means that something is causing a bad effect and someone wants to change the situation. This change may be either through private means or from government.

This stage strives to address such questions as:

- What is the problem?

- Where does it exist?
- Who or what is affected?
- How did it develop?
- What are the major causes?
- How might the causes be affected by policy action?

Analysts therefore need to describe the set of conditions, usually through the collection of relevant facts or data on its magnitude or extent. For example, who is affected by it and how seriously are they affected? How long has the situation existed and how might it change over the next several years or decades? How possible is it to address the problem through one means or another? The goals and objectives of such means, also known as interventions may not be clear to all concerned, whether private or governmental (see Box 3-1).

The danger that cell phones pose when used by drivers is a good example of a problem to be analyzed. The analyst may ask how cell phone use is related to auto accidents. Other questions might involve how accident rates can be reduced through policy action or how cell phone use compares to other driving distractions, such as passenger distractions, the radio, drinking coffee, and applying make up.

It may also be necessary to clarify what is the meant by the set of conditions, to define it clearly, and to develop accurate measures of it. If the problem is homelessness, for example, an analyst would need to be clear about what is meant by homelessness, how to determine the extent of it, and who is affected by it. Does the definition only include people who sleep on the streets and in train stations? Does it include people who are off the streets and in temporary shelters? Is it broad enough to include people who are living with friends or family on a temporary basis, but have no permanent home to go to? What percent of the homeless are women? How many are young people, middle aged, and old? Why are they homeless? How many have problems with alcohol? How many have problems with mental illness? How many just need a job? For most public problems, analysts will want to develop quantitative measures of this kind.

In addition to gathering basic information about the problem, analysts want to identify its causes. This is not always an easy task. Without a good idca of how and why the problem developed, however, it is difficult to think usefully about possible solutions. This kind of diagnosis of the problem is very much like what a physician does when a patient is sick or what a mechanic does when a car is not running properly.

The importance of diagnosis is clear when you look at how policy makers are trying to cope with an issue as large as global terrorism. Without understanding the causes of terrorism, policy actions are unlikely to be effective. Even if they are understood, they may be too numerous to address. A more common issue is education reform. Before deciding what should be done, policy makers must decide what the problem is and what its causes are. Otherwise, there is little reason to believe that specific actions will improve the quality of schools.

Construct Policy Alternatives

Constructing policy alternatives may be the most important stage in the policy analysis process. If analysts and policy makers cannot think of creative ways to solve problems, conventional approaches that may no longer be appropriate will continue. Early in the process, therefore, analysts need to think imaginatively and critically about how the problem might be addressed, both within government and outside it.

[Box 3-2] ***Problems versus Issues***

Policy problems are really whole systems of problems. Therefore, policy issues must be equally complex. Policy issues are not only disagreements about actual or potential courses of action. They also reflect competing views of the nature of the problems themselves. Policy issues are therefore the result of prior disputes about the definition, classification, explanation, and evaluation of problems. An apparently clear-cut policy issue – for example, whether the government should enforce air quality standards in industry – is typically the consequence of conflicting sets of assumptions about the nature of pollution:

1. Pollution is a natural consequence of capitalism, an economic system where the owners of industry seek to maintain and increase profits from their investments. Some damage to the environment is a necessary price to pay for a healthy capitalist economy.
2. Pollution is a result of the need for power and prestige among industrial managers who seek promotions in large career-oriented bureaucracies. Pollution is just as severe in socialist systems where there are no profit-seeking private owners.
3. Pollution is a consequence of consumer preferences in mass-consumption society. In order to ensure corporate survival owners and managers must satisfy consumer preferences for high-performance engines

and automobile travel.

The ability to recognize differences among problematic situations, policy problems, and policy issues is crucial for understanding the different ways that common experiences are translated into disagreements about actual and potential courses of government action. The formulation of a problem is heavily influenced by the assumptions that different policy stakeholders – legislators, agency administrators, business leaders, consumer groups – bring to a given problem situation. In turn, different formulations of the problem shape the ways that policy issues are defined. In the above example of environmental pollution, assumptions about the operation of a healthy capitalist economy result in a negative position on government enforcement of air quality standards in industry, while assumptions about corporate managerial behavior are likely to result in an affirmative position. By contrast, the third set of assumptions about consumer preferences and corporate survival may produce the position that government regulation of industrial pollution is not an issue. This is because government cannot legislate consumer demand.

In sum, this stage asks the question of what policy options might be considered for dealing with the problem.

One approach that has gained increasing acceptance is privatization, the transfer of public services from government to the private sector. Such private sector solutions, recommended by many policy analysts and organizations, and sometimes endorsed by government, are said to be more appealing, and perhaps more effective, than reliance on a government agency. Education is divided between public and private schools. Many people support privatization of the national pension system. Many services are also provided by public corporations, instead of directly by the government. The search for possible policy alternatives can produce new ideas that gain a measure of public acceptance.

Returning to the example of auto accidents caused by drivers distracted by cell phones, three possible alternatives to consider would be whether government should make fines to reduce drivers' cell phone use, if government should try to educate drivers about cell phone use, and whether or not it would be technologically feasible to disable cell phones in a moving car.

Choose the Evaluative Criteria

When the policy alternatives have been identified, the analysis shifts to assessing their potential. This task calls for deciding on suitable criteria for evaluation. There are many appropriate criteria, such as political feasibility, administrative feasibility, technical feasibility, environmental impacts, ethical considerations, and political values, which can be used to assess policy proposals. Even though the list of potential evaluative criteria might look long, some criteria will be more appropriate than others for any particular problem.

This stage comes down to the following questions:

- What criteria are most suitable for the problem and the alternatives?
- What are the costs of action or inaction?
- What is the likely effectiveness?

- What is the social and political feasibility?
- How equitable is the alternative?

For example, the Sunshine Policy has been under attack from conservatives in Korea. The new government of Lee Myungbak has referred to the policies of the previous Noh and Kim governments as "ten lost years" (see Box 3-3). On what basis should analysts evaluate changes to the policy, particularly in relation to other national security issues? One criterion would have to be the relative costs and benefits. Another might be what is politically possible, given the preferences of the Korean public. How would an analysis go about determining the answer?

[Box 3-3] ***Lee Myungbak and the Sunshine Policy***

The Sunshine Policy inaugurated by President Kim Daejung and continued under Noh Moohyun was not greeted well by conservatives. Accustomed to hostility and conflict with the North, the Korean right preferred to align with the American right and continue pressure on the North, calling the ten years of the two centrist presidents "ten lost years" on the subject of North Korea policy.

Conservatives tended to oppose the policy as being pro-North, emphasizing a national security approach instead. They also cited the lack of practical results for all of the aid South Korea had spent on the North. This is in stark contrast to more liberal approaches that either saw the policy in drawing the North into engagement with the South or simply as humanitarian aid.

Lee Myungbak moved to implement the conservative agenda by placing stiff conditions on aid to the North. His policy was almost immediately undermined by agreement between the US and North Korea over dismantling the North's nuclear program. Lee's policy was also undermined by massive public protests. *Hankyoreh* reported on June 21, 2008 as the candlelight rallies entered their 51st day the hope of finding ways of improving inter-Korean relations was fading. They quoted an unnamed government official who said, "It will likely take some time (to normalize inter-Korean relations)."

Discussion Questions

- What are the purposes of the Sunshine Policy?
- How should the government deal with North Korea?
- What are the most important factors in dealing with the North? Humanitarian aid? National Reconciliation? Human rights? National Security?
- Will South Korea be able to resume the Sunshine Policy?

– Hankyoreh Media Company

Plenty of information is available about the Sunshine Policy, but a good deal of it is contradictory, and the analysts disagree heatedly about the core issues, such as costs and benefits. Conservatives have stressed economic and political costs, while liberals have stressed values. Nevertheless, policymakers and analysts need to ask the questions and try to find answers. Students of public policy need to be aware of different criteria and be prepared to think about which criteria are best suited to making the correct choices for society, because multiple criteria almost always exist for evaluating policy proposals.

For some policy actions, as with the Sunshine Policy, the evaluative criteria will likely include political values. National security will be weighed against other needs, such as promoting national reconciliation. As this example indicates, there may be conflicts between criteria. Free trade agreements raise similar questions. On what basis should policy analysts, citizens, and policymakers judge the suitability of policy options, such as concessions in some areas in order to win an overall agreement? Are the costs of sacrificing some economic interests worth the gains to other sectors, not to mention overall gains?

Going back to the cell phone usc regulation example, we may ask what the most important criteria for regulating cell phones are, what options might be most effective, whether the options are socially acceptable, and whether or not it would ethical to restrict individual behavior to achieve this social goal.

Assess the Alternatives

At this stage analysts ask which of the alternatives that might be considered seriously is most likely to produce the outcome sought. This is true whether it is to improve economic growth, improve the plight of the homeless, raise educational quality, or protect the environment. This exercise involves making judgments about how well each policy option fits in relation to the most relevant criteria. The analysts can rank the options in terms of overall desirability or they may consider the options in terms of each criterion, such as effectiveness, cost, and equity.

Some specialists refer to this stage of the process as projecting the outcomes or assessing impacts. A number of different methods or tools are used to do this. Cost-benefit analysis, cost-effectiveness, risk assessment, decision analysis, forecasting, impact assessment, and ethical analysis are among the most common methods of analysis.

The basic questions asked by the analyst at this stage include:

- Which alternatives are better than others?
- What kind of analysis might help to distinguish policy alternatives?
- Is the evidence available(If not, how can it be produced?)?

Analysts have many ways of presenting alternatives so that policymakers and other interested people and groups can understand the analysis and the choices they face. For example, if three policy options are offered for consideration, the analyst might present each in terms of its likely effectiveness, economic efficiency, and equity. Tradeoffs are inevitable in this kind of decision making. Only rarely does a given policy option rank highest on all of the evaluative criteria. It is far more likely that one option is judged to be most effective, but another is cheaper or more equitable in its effects. Analysts, therefore, try to resolve this difficulty by attaching weight to each of the criteria.

For example, is equity more important than efficiency in improving the national economy? Should government try to help the most disadvantaged citizens first or try to improve economic conditions? Should the government think about jobs first and only about overall growth rates after more jobs have been created? Would doing so promote greater equity? As analysts consider more than a few conflicting bases for assessing policy options, the necessity for weighting criteria increases.

From the cell phone accident example, the analyst might ask if fines or education would be more likely to reduce drivers' cell phone use. The analyst could also look at how successful government efforts to regulate cell phone use have been. Finally, the analysts would consider what evidence would be needed to answer these questions.

Draw Conclusions

Analysts summarize their findings and draw conclusions about the relative merits of competing policy proposals. However, they leave the choice of policy action to policymakers and the public. Whichever approach is taken, one must bear in mind that all analysis is limited. Analysis can never be complete. It cannot cover every possible question or address every contingency. It also cannot be free of limitations because every method or tool that might be used has some constraints. Policy analysts need to develop a strong ability to deal with uncertainty, which is part of the process of policy analysis.

The questions the analyst ponders at this stage are which policy option is the most desirable given the circumstances and the evaluative criteria and what other factors should be considered.

Concluding the example of addressing the problem of cell phone use causing car accidents, an analyst considering recommending fines should ask whether government should impose stiff fines, would such fines be accepted as legitimate and how any action might be made more acceptable.

Sometimes it may be difficult to draw a conclusion. In that case students of policy analysis are advised to learn to ask critical questions about the information they collect, especially regarding its validity.

Some of the relevant questions are:

- Where did the information come from, and how reliable is the source?
- Is there any way to double-check the facts and the interpretation of them?
- Does the information and analysis seem to be believable?
- Are there any signs of bias that might affect the conclusions that the study offers?
- If two or more studies contradict one another, what are the reasons?
- Are differences due to political ideologies, differences in the preferred policy actions, or differences in the way the problem is defined?
- Are the authors too selective in deciding what information should be presented and what can be left out?

By gathering information from multiple sources and comparing different interpretations, students might find it easier to determine which of the studies is the most credible.

Discussion Questions

1. What are the components of policy analysis?
2. Which kind of policy analysis is the most useful? Why do you prefer that type?
3. Provide an example of the policy analysis steps using a real world problem.
4. How are problems different from issues?

Vocabulary

outcomes	diagnosis
alternatives	define
monitoring	analyze
scientific analysis	evaluative
practical interference	criteria
professional analysis	problem
problem structuring	issue
political analysis	equity
think tank	Sunshine Policy

References

Anderson, James E. (2003). *Public Policymaking,* 5th ed. Houghton Mifflin: Boston, MA.

·Bardach, Eugene (2000). *A Practical Guide for Policy Analysis: The Eightfold Path to More Effective Problem Solving* Chatham House: New York, NY.

Kingdon, John W. (1995). *Agendas, Alternatives, and Public Policies,* 2nd ed. Harper Collins College: New York, NY.

"Korea, U.S. Close to Beef Agreement" http://english.chosun.com/w21data/html/news/200804/200804170015.html

Kraft, E. Michael, and Furlong, R. Scott (2004). *Public Policy: Politics, Analysis, and Alternatives.* CQ Press: Washington, DC.

Lindblom, Charles E., and Woodhouse, Edward J. (1993). *The Policy-Making Process.* 3rd ed. Prentice Hall: Upper Saddle River, NJ.

MacRae, Duncan, Whittington, Dale (1997). *Expert Advice for Policy Choice.* Georgetown University Press: Washington, DC.

"New Beef Agreement Still Leaves Room for Mad Cow Fears" http://english. hani.co.kr/arti/english_edition/e_national/294857.html

Patton, Carl V., and Sawicki, David S. (1993). *Basic Methods of Policy Analysis and Planning,* 2nd ed. Prentice Hall: Englewood Cliffs, NJ.

"S. Korea's Policy on North Becoming Tougher" http://english.hani.co.kr/arti/english_edition/e_northkorea/294560.html

Stone, Deborah (2002). *Policy Paradox: The Art of Political Decisionmaking.* W.W. Norton: New York, NY.

Weimer, L. David, and Vining, R. Aidan (2005). *Policy Analysis: Concepts and Practice.* Pearson Prentice Hall: Englewood [liffs, NJ.

Weiss, Carol H. (1992). *Organizations for Policy Analysis: Helping Government Think.* Sage: Newbury Park, CA.

"Where's the Beef?" http://www.thenation.com/doc/20080707/cumings

WEEK 4 Problem Analysis

Summary
Problem description means identifying causes, determining the nature of the problem, its severity, where and how often it occurs, how new it is, how critical it is, the characteristics of the affected population, the orientation of the definer, and the nature of the solution.

The nature of the problem is defined through various statistics and measures. There may be different definitions, the problem may be seen as belonging to different paradigms, and it may be seen as having different levels of severity. Policy arguments often depend on operational measures of a problem. Statistical information is useful and often widely available to define and assist with analysis, although not all data can be quantified. Forecasting is a way of looking for future trends.

Problem analysis includes defining, measuring, determining the extent and magnitude, and causes of a problem while setting goals and objectives for a solution and determining what can be done.

Policy studies usually focus on proximate causes, but may also address root causes. Most problems have multiple causes and thus many different possible solutions that must be weighed according to their respective costs and benefits.

The beginning of any policy study involves the description of a problem. Sometimes the problem is obvious. Sometimes its causes are even obvious. For example, if the problem is teenage smoking and how to curtail it, it is possible to find abundant information about why teenagers smoke and how many of them there are. Knowing their numbers, it is easy to determine the implications of lifelong smoking habits for associated health problems.

[Figure 4-1] Doctor Examining a Patient

The process of policy analysis is very much like the process of medicine. The analyst takes apart and examines the issue, defines and diagnoses the problem, and comes up with a range of practical solutions.

This example shows how simple some kinds of problem analysis can be. The problems can be straightforward, and the information needed to make a policy choice is available, thanks to national surveys that collect it.

Problem analysis involves trying to answer the basic questions about problems. These questions include:

- What is the nature of the problem?
- What is the magnitude or extent of the problem?
- How did the problem start or develop?
- What are the problem's major causes?
- Why is it important to deal with the problem as a matter of public policy?
- What does the problem entail?
- What is already known about the problem?
- What are the possible solutions?

This process requires students of public policy to think critically and creatively about the problem.

[Table 4-1] Problem Description

Dimensions of Problem Description	
Problem Dimensions	Options
Cause of Problem	· personal or impersonal · intended or accidental · blame allocated or blame avoided · simple or complex
Nature of the Problem	
Severity	· degrees of severity
Incidence	· growing, stable or declining · social patterns: by class, population, age, gender, etc.

Novelty	· unprecedented or familiar
Proximity	· personally relevant or a general social concern
Crisis	· crisis or non-crisis · emergency or non-emergency
Characteristics of the Problem Population	· deserving or undeserving · familiar or strange · sympathetic or threatening
Ends/Means Orientation of Problem Definer	· instrumental or expressive
Nature of the Solution	· available or nonexistent · acceptable or objectionable · affordable or unaffordable

11 The Nature of Problems

The first step in policy making is to define and analyze the problem. Problem analysis involves trying to answer the basic questions about the nature of the problem, its extent or magnitude, how it came about, what its major causes are, and why it is important to deal with it as a matter of public policy.

Definitions and Measures

Any copy of the daily newspaper contains information about a large number of potential policy problems: crime, pollution, inflation, energy, welfare, unemployment, and many more. These are all problems. Few people will say that they are not. Each of these conditions interferes with the attainment of some value or need. They may interfere with personal security, health, consumption or some other value or need. Yet this everyday understanding of the meaning of what makes a problem is frequently inadequate for policy purposes. This is because it obscures the fact that the same problem is viewed in radically different ways by different segments of the population. Take the example of crime. For some, crime is a natural condition of all human societies while for others it is an understandable response to poverty and exploitation.

The way we view crime as a problem depends on several factors:

First, different people may agree that crimc is a problem, but disagree about the kinds of behaviors that are criminal. One person may define crime solely in terms of violent acts against people (homicide, armed robbery, rape) (see Box 4-1). Another person may focus on illegal acts involving property (theft, fraud, embezzlement, government corruption).

Second, people may also disagree about the kind or class of problems that are criminal. Some people see crime as an economic problem. To them, a potential resolution lies in restructuring the production and distribution of goods and services in society. Others see it as a social, psychological, or administrative problem which may be resolved by providing greater opportunities for social mobility, by changing attitudes through education, or by strictly enforcing current criminal laws. Generally, the way people classify a problem determines the way they will explain and attempt to resolve it.

Finally, people may agree on the definition, classification, and explanation of a problem. Even after that they may yet disagree about its scope, severity, and importance. Judgments about the severity of a problem depend largely on what values and needs are deemed to be most important. Persons with a strong need for physical security or those who are committed to values of law and order are more likely to view crime as a policy problem than those with a strong commitment to social justice.

However, an essential step in the policy process is to define the problem. Definitions make it possible for those seeking a solution to communicate with one another with a degree of precision that otherwise might not be possible. For example, if analysts are studying the plight of the poor, they need to define what poverty means. Is being poor only a matter of having insufficient money or income? Does it include other characteristics, such as the lack of certain skills or abilities? Should poverty be defined in relative terms or in absolute terms? Is there a culture of poverty?

Public policy arguments also depend on operational measures or operational indicators of problems. Rather than refer to poverty in the abstract, analysts want to know how many people live in poverty and their demographics. If discussing educational quality in the public schools, analysts want to see test scores and other student evaluations to determine if a problem exists in the schools and how one community's schools compare to another's. If the subject is violent crime, the analysts need statistics about the number of crimes committed nationally and in local communities, and whether the crime rate is increasing or decreasing.

Quantitative measures are abundant for most contemporary public problems. How much statistical information needs to be provided is a matter of judgment. At a minimum, most issue papers or problems analyses include basic descriptive statistics. One descriptive type is the frequency count, such as the percentage of the population at different income levels or the number of people in a survey who respond one way or another.

Another type is the mean (average) measure of a group or category, such as the average score on an examination. An alternative is the median of a variable, which is the point where one half of the group lies above and one half below. One example is the median price of apartments sold in different regions of the nation. Some idea of the range of variation or the correlation or relationship between two variables, such as gender and income, may be useful as well.

Statistical information can be displayed in many ways in a report. These include tables that show frequency counts or percentages of what is being studied, such as the percentage of different age groups in the homeless population. Information can be superimposed on maps to show geographic variations such as rates of urban growth or the income levels for adjacent urban and suburban areas. Graphic figures, like pie charts or bar charts, are common. Line figures, such as the number of people without children from 1970 to 2005, that show how the magnitude of a problem changes over time, are also common.

There is an art to choosing how best to display quantitative information. Reports should at least aim for clarity. Some visual displays are also more likely to capture the reader's attention than others. The use of computer-generated color graphics allows a range of different formats, both in written form and in a PowerPoint or similar presentation. The best advice generally is to keep the audience and purpose clearly in mind when choosing the format of a report or presentation. The use of quantitative data also carries some risks. Analysts need to be aware of the possibility of inaccurate data in a report or an invalid measurement that does not truly explain the problem.

Naturally, not all human concerns, such as happiness or the sense of well-being, can be reduced to quantitative measures.

Analysts can, however, make use of surveys that ask people whether they are happy, enjoying living in their communities, believe the schools are doing a good job, and so forth. Where a public problem cannot be measured directly, this kind of survey may be a useful substitute. Economists also say that people can be asked to estimate the monetary value of many activities for which no market value exists. Their responses can help to calculate whether certain actions, such as preserving open space or planting trees, are justifiable uses of tax money.

Anticipating the Future

One other aspect of defining and measuring problems deserves mention. Any consideration of the present state of affairs must be grounded in an assessment of how it is likely to change over time. What will the problem look like in several years or decades? Forecasts, also known as projections, usually involve an extrapolation of current trends, but that is only one method for looking ahead to the future.

Examples of forecasting include economic forecasting (will the nation have a surplus or deficit in five years?), population projections (how large will the country's population be by 2025 or 2050?), and energy needs (what kind, how much, and where?). Such projections are especially helpful if they reveal how that change will likely happen with or without policy intervention. For example, if the nation adopted energy conservation measures, how much would that action reduce the reliance on imported oil?

12 Major Components of Problem Analysis

The flow chart in Figure 4-2 summarizes the basic elements in problem analysis. The list can also be a guide to what questions might be addressed in preparing a problem analysis or issue paper.

Define the Problem

If the problem is educational quality, what does that mean? What is the exact nature of the education problem under the study? Has quality declined? Is it lower than many people believe it ought to be? Is it lower in Korea than in other developed nations?

[Figure 4-2] Problem Analysis Flow Chart

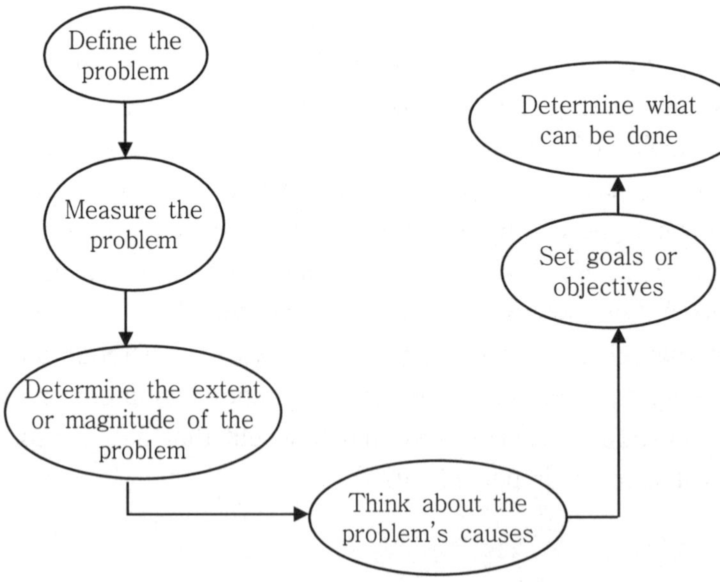

Measure the Problem

Find a way to measure the problem that is consistent with the way it is defined. This step is sometimes called developing an operational definition. What kinds of quantitative indicators are available from reliable sources? What is the best measurement to use for educational quality? Should it be student scores on standardized examinations? Should there be other measures of student learning? Instead, should we use indicators of the quality of a school's faculty?

Determine the Extent or Magnitude of the Problem

Using indicators that are available, try to determine who is affected by the problem and by how much. Try to answer these kinds of questions. What groups in the population suffer from the problem being studied, how long have they been affected by it, and to what extent are they affected? For example, how does educational quality vary from one city or province to another, from urban districts to rural districts or from schools in less-affluent neighborhoods to those in more-affluent areas?

Think about the Problem's Causes

How did the problem come about, and why does it continue? What are the leading causes of the problem, and what other causes should be considered? Knowing the causes of a problem is critical to developing solutions to it. How has educational quality changed over the past several decades, and why? Why has sex crime increased among Korean youth (see Box 4-1)?

[Box 4-1] *Sex Crimes Increasing among Korean Youth*

The number of Korean teenagers involved in acts of serious sexual violence like rape has risen significantly in the last two years, according to statistics from the Ministry of Education, Science and Technology, as reported by *Chosun Ilbo*.

Statistics show that the number of victims of rape or sexual assault under the age of 20 has increased an amazing 44% percent over the past two years. The number of teenage attackers in such cases has gone up 60%.

The number of teenage victims has been increasing, from 3,787 in 2005 to 5,159 in 2006 and to 5,460 in 2007. Teenage offenders under 20 years of age increased from 1,329 in 2005 to 1,811 in 2006 up to 2,136 in 2007.

Some factors experts and the government have cited in explaining this increase in crime include a superficial sex education curriculum and a lack of professional personnel conducting such classes as well as easy access to pornography through the internet and cable television as partially responsible for the increase in sexual crimes. Some observers have also said that the lack of serious punishment, even for repeat offenders, plays a role.

Discussion Questions

- How serious is this increase in youth sex crime?
- How much effort should the police and courts devote towards this class of crime compared with other crimes?
- What are the causes? Are there different proximate and root causes?
- How can this problem be addressed by government?

– Chosun Ilbo

Set Goals or Objectives

What should be done about the problem and why? Are certain goals and objectives the most important, widely accepted, and economically or socially feasible? Over what period of time should the goals and objectives be sought? For educational quality, what goals or objectives are most appropriate? If quality is to be improved, how much progress should be expected for a given period of time?

Determine What Can Be Done

What actions might solve the problem or at least reach the specified goals and objectives? What policy efforts might be directed at the causes of the problem? What variables can be affected by such efforts? If the goal is improving educational quality to a certain extent, what needs to be done? How do we improve teacher quality, reduce class size, or change the curriculum? All of these are common concerns of educational reform, and are very practical problems.

13 Problem Causes and Solutions

Any assessment of a public problem requires thinking about its causes. Analysts also need to consider how it came about and why it continues. The answers make a big difference in whether and how public policy might resolve the problem. For example, if the question is why prison populations increased dramatically from 2000 to 2005 in Korea, part of the answer is that the poor economic conditions led to fewer jobs being created for younger workers while older workers were often laid off early before retirement. More of these workers responded by committing survival-related crimes to get by. Some of them even tried to get caught so that they could get food and shelter in jail. Instead of paying money for automobile accidents, some preferred to go to jail where they could at least earn some money.

Most policy studies focus on what can be called proximate, or immediate, causes of public problems, such as the reasons for rising prison populations. The greater challenge is to deal with the root causes of problems. Taking policy action might be more difficult because of long-standing public attitudes and habits that are resistant to change. Think about urban traffic congestion. Why does it exist? The obvious answer is that too many people are driving their cars on a limited number of roads at the same time. Is the solution to build more highways? On the other hand, could the solution be to think about ways to reduce the use of automobile in urban areas where and when congestion is greatest? Some urban designers and environmentalists offer a more radical solution, at least for new cities. They suggest building cities with adequate mass transit and where people can live closer to where they work. Many cities are adopting sustainable policies and Local Agenda 21 with similar ambitions for managing anticipated growth over the next several decades.

Most public problems have multiple causes. As a result, people disagree over which is the most important and which ought to be the object of public policy. The good student of public policy learns how to deal with the politics and often overheated rhetoric that can sometimes distort an objective review of the evidence.

Problem analysis can begin by making an explicit list of the goals and objectives of the various policy actors. Then there can be a determination of what might be done to reach those goals and objectives. The objectives might include a specific measure of what is to be achieved, such as improving the economic growth rate or improving relations with North Korea. When analysts think of potential solutions to public problems, they try to identify the opportunities for policy intervention. They try to imagine how a change in public policy might affect the problem. For example, would lowering corporate tax rates increase job growth?

Sometimes analysts want to describe the benefits and costs of trying to solve the problem. They look at how the consequences of policy action are distributed across different populations. Those in certain regions, occupations, or social groups may experience different effects from both positive and negative consequences. Different groups gain and lose when a problem is resolved. Politicians and other major policy actors are sometimes very clever about addressing these kinds of distributive concerns. They are almost always interested in knowing about them. They may speak about solving public problems as though the entire nation will benefit equally, but the reality is that some segments of the population are more likely than others to enjoy the benefits of acting on a problem, and some are more likely than others to pay the costs. As a student of public policy it would be wise to think about how to present such information in any studies.

Discussion Questions

1. What questions are necessary for describing problems?
2. Give a real example that shows the difficulty of defining problems for policy analysis.
3. Why are specific measures of problems important to problem definition?
4. Why is it necessary to consider the future in policy analysis?
5. How necessary is it to consider the future in policy analysis?
6. How possible is it to determine all the causes of a problem? How necessary is it?

Vocabulary

causation
clarity
forecasting
magnitude
severity
incidence
novelty
proximity
projection
crisis
quantitative
statistical
objective
operational definition
operational indicator
operational measure
quantitative measure

References

Kingdon, John W. (1995). *Agendas, Alternatives, and Public Policies,* 2nd ed. Harper Collins College: New York, NY.

Kraft, E. Michael, and Furlong, R. Scott (2004). *Public Policy: Politics, Analysis, and Alternatives.* CQ Press: Washington, DC.

Miringhoff, Marc, and Miringhoff, Marque-Luisa (1999). *Social Health of the Nation: How America is Really Doing.* Oxford: New York, NY.

Patton, Carl V., and Sawicki, David S. (1993). *Basic Methods of Policy Analysis and Planning,* 2nd ed. Prentice Hall: Englewood Cliffs, NJ.

"Sex Crimes Among Korean Youth on the Rise" http://english. chosun.com/ w21data/ html/news/200805/200805130024.html

Stone, Deborah (2002). *Policy Paradox: The Art of Political Decision-making.* W.W. Norton: New York, NY.

WEEK 5 Information and Alternatives

Summary

There are many useful sources of information, including websites, journal articles, books, magazines and newspapers, literature reviews, and interviews of policy actors. Policy-relevant information may address problems, alternatives, actions, outcomes, and performance. Gathering information requires interpretation. Policy-relevant information varies widely in quality and usefulness. It is often misleading and must always be read critically, regardless of source.

Analysts may go beyond policy typologies and variations on existing policies. They may also gather ideas through brainstorming. They may do quick surveys. They may conduct literature reviews to discover what is known about a problem. They may also compare existing situations against some ideal standard.

In order to have options to consider, policy analysts must construct alternatives. There are many different kinds of things that governments can do as part of policy. Governments may regulate, subsidize, ration, tax and spend, contract out, use market incentives, privatize, charge fees, educate, create public trusts, and conduct research. Institutional reform and reorganization is yet another possibility. Policies use agents to affect the target population, two kinds of policy actors. Agents affect target populations through using policy tools. There are five types of policy tools. They are authority tools, inducements and sanctions, capacity-building tools, hortatory tools, and learning tools.

14 Sources of Information

Gathering reliable information is necessary for performing problem analysis and other activities related to it. Good information is critical to successful analysis.

Where can and should analysts go to look for and to find information? The following list of sources may be of some help:

- Websites, including from government agencies
- Articles in academic journals
- Books on the subject
- Newspapers and professional news weeklies
- Visits to government and other relevant offices
- Interviews of policy actors
- Literature review

Websites

Most university libraries have a variety of internet search tools available that can greatly simplify an information search. Your favorite web search engine can return many useful links for specific public policy analysis. Online databases often contain full-text articles and can be searched by subject matter, title, or by author. Card catalogs, generally online today, can be searched in the same way. For example, to identify articles or reports on public satisfaction or dissatisfaction with healthcare, use Naver, Daum, or Google or similar search engines by typing in the keywords "healthcare," "public satisfaction," and "complaints" to find a suitable list of studies and public opinion surveys. To vary the search, as in to find material on whether patients believe it is difficult to obtain referrals to medical specialist, add or substitute keywords such as "cost," "patients," and "specialists."

[Figure 5-1] Searching on the Internet for Policy Information

Books on the Subject

Books on related subjects may some of the best sources for collecting information. They may be available in university libraries, public libraries, and commercial libraries.

Newspapers and Professional News Weeklies

Newspapers and news weeklies provide valuable information about current policy debates, particularly on a national level, and some background on the nature of the problem.

Visits to Government and Other Relevant Offices and Interview Policy Actors

To gather information, arranging to visit government and other relevant offices as well as interviews with policy actors is useful. Especially at the local level, policy makers and other actors often welcome a visit by someone who is interested in what they are doing. Advance preparation is essential for this strategy. Analysts should know what information they are seeking and who is most likely to be able to provide it. Reading a local newspaper for coverage of the issue is a good place to start the search.

Visit Government Agency Websites

Visiting websites for the government agencies most directly related to the issue is another way to locate pertinent information. The National Assembly, Cheongwadae, and all of the various government ministries all maintain websites accessible to the public.

Literature Review

When analysts must determine what else they need to know to complete the assessment, then a literature search could be useful for seeking more detailed sources of information.

How much information is enough? The main concern at this point of a search is to find enough information to understand the basics about a given policy problem. If the initial search yields three or four high-quality articles that give a basic idea of the history of the problem and policy efforts and controversies, it may be enough. As long as the information covers the different major points of view about desirable policy actions it should help policy analysts proceed to deepen their understanding of an issue.

15 Policy-Relevant Information

Figure 5-2 gives us a clear picture of the types and categories of policy-relevant information.

[Figure 5-2] Types of Policy-Relevant Information

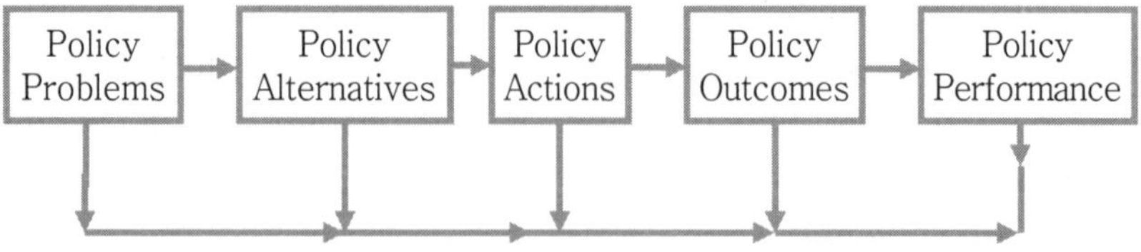

A policy problem is a value, need, or opportunity which may be attained through public action. However it is defined, knowledge of what problem to solve requires information about a problem's antecedent conditions (for example, school dropouts as an antecedent condition of unemployment). An antecedent is simply something that comes before something else. It may or may not be a cause, but it certainly is an indicator. Information about values (for example, better schools or full employment) whose attainment may lead to a problem's solution is a good example of necessary information. The provision of information about policy problems is the most critical task of policy analysis, since the way a problem is defined governs our ability to search out and identify appropriate solutions. Inadequate or faulty information at this stage of analysis may result in a fatal error. It may result in solving the wrong formulation of a problem.

A policy alternative is a potentially available course of action that may contribute to the attainment of values and, as a result, the resolution of a policy problem. Information about the conditions that gave rise to a problem is essential to the identification of possible solutions. Yet such information is not usually enough. The past may not repeat itself, while values themselves change over time. For these reasons the analyst must be concerned with producing information about alternatives that are not necessarily provided by the existing solutions. To produce such information requires creativity, insight, and what many have called intuition, judgment, or tacit knowledge.

A policy action is a move or series of moves guided by a policy alternative that is designed to achieve valued outcomes. In order to recommend or advocate consequences of acting on different alternatives, including information about the political, legal, and economic constraints on action. Yet it is also essential to know which alternative courses of action are preferable on evaluative grounds. It is also necessary to get information about which policy alternatives are valued and why. Therefore, information about policy actions is produced by forecasting and evaluating the expected consequences of actions. Policy recommendation presupposes monitoring, forecasting, and evaluation.

A policy outcome is an observed consequence of policy actions. The consequences of policy actions cannot be fully stated or known in advance. Not all observed consequences of action are intended or anticipated. Policy analysis therefore produces information about policy actions both before and after they have occurred.

Policy performance is the degree to which a given policy outcome contributes to the attainment of values. In reality policy problems are seldom solved. They are most often resolved, reformulated, or even unsolved. For this reason policy analysis is best described as a methodology for problem structuring and not as a means for solving problems. Yet to know whether a problem has been solved, resolved, or unsolved does not only require information about policy outcomes. It is also essential to know whether these outcomes have contributed to the attainment of values that originally gave rise to a problem. Information about policy performance, which is evaluative in character, may be used to develop new policy alternatives or to restructure policy problems.

16 Challenges of Gathering Information

The interpretation of the gathered information is one of the most challenging aspects of a literature review. As this text has emphasized earlier, policy analyses vary greatly in quality and are often prepared for use to advance one side in policy debates, with selective and sometimes misleading summaries and commentaries. Researchers need to have media literacy, the knowledge of how to consume and understand media. Just because a statement appears in print or on the web is no guarantee that it is true. This is very true in the internet age where it is easy to distribute incorrect information. Some groups do this for political purposes (see Box 5-1). It is always essential to find out the sources of information, the reliability of authors or organizations. Media literacy also requires looking for any critical assumptions that are made in a study or report, such as what is included and what is omitted, and any interpretations that might not be justified. At a minimum, the researcher will want to determine whether the facts are current and accurate.

[Box 5-1] *Information Distortion: Intentional or Honest Mistake?*

A translator for the MBC news program PD Notebook says its April 29, 2008 broadcast intentional distortions. The translator says she made it clear it was unfair to depict footage of a downer cow taken by an animal rights group as showing a cow "possibly" stricken by mad cow disease, but she claims such concerns fell on deaf ears. She added the proper way of handling the death of the young Virginia woman, which PD Notebook depicted as having died from variant Creutzfeldt-Jakob Disease, or the human form of mad cow disease, would have been to clearly mention that it was by no means certain she had vCJD (which she did not have-only one American has contracted vCJD, from eating British beef while living in England).

She said the distortion of facts committed by PD Notebook was not due to a problem in translation, but a specific goal in the production and editing of the news program. She urged the producers of the program to admit their bias in handling that report. The program helped encourage massive protests by spreading exaggerated fears about mad cow disease based on false information.

PD Notebook blamed its translators, saying they had created room for misunderstanding due to "liberal" translation.

Mcanwhile, prosecutors have begun investigating the broad-cast, along with the possibility for charging the program with libel. The conservative media call this a simple prosecution for libel, asserting that facts are important. On the other hand, the liberal media are calling it an attack on free speech, saying that the issues should be addressed at MBC.

Meanwhile, in a case that was not investigated or prosecuted, a former agriculture minister accused the US government in a magazine article of concealing the results of tests by Yale University and the University of Pittsburgh showing that at least 250,000 to 650,000 people in the United States had died from the human form of mad cow disease but this was being covered up as deaths from senile dementia. The Yale and University of Pittsburgh research papers cited by Kim actually said that from 5% to 13% of senile dementia patients in the United States may suffer from standard Creutzfeldt Jakob Disease (CJD), which has no relation to beef or mad cow disease.

Discussion Questions

- What is the responsibility of the press to provide accurate information? What should be done when it does not?

- What is the difference between intentional and mistaken distortion?
- Under American libel law, a lie must cause damage and be proven intentional. Under British law, it must be proven to have caused harm. The US has much freer speech, but sometimes the press goes too far. The UK has more accurate reporting, but it sometimes does not report things it "knows" because they are difficult to prove to be true. Which standard is the most appropriate?
- What is the difference between the case of the television program that was prosecuted and the case of the magazine article? Should they both be prosecuted? Should neither be prosecuted?

– *Chosun Ilbo*, Hankyoreh Media Company

The real excitement in policy studies comes from having strong interest in a particular policy area and learning where to find the information about it. For example, the student who is passionate about unequal pay for women in the workforce will find the search for appropriate data and studies exciting. For the researcher concerned about declining opportunities to download music and videos from the internet, the hunt for information about copyright laws and restrictions on using downloaded files will be easy and a real learning experience.

Analysts can try other techniques in addition to considering standard policy types or variations on existing policies to expand the list of alternatives. This week is about how to apply creative thinking to policy. This is a process of increasing options and alternatives so that the policy analyst and, ultimately, the decision makers and the public have more choices. Here, it is hoped, a broader and more vibrant debate will ensue, resulting in better consideration of available options. More debate, more options, along with more creativity can lead to better decisions.

There are many creative approaches to policy making. Some of the common strategies that have been suggested include no-action analysis, quick surveys, literature reviews, comparison to real world situations, passive collection and classification, use of analogies and metaphors, brainstorming, and comparison with an ideal. Four of the most common and most useful approaches for students are:

- Brainstorming
- Quick surveys
- Literature reviews
- Comparison with an ideal

17 Brainstorming

Brainstorming is a method for generating ideas, goals, and strategies that help identify and conceptualize problematic situations. It may be used to generate a large number of suggestions about potential solutions for problems.

Brainstorming is a popular technique to encourage creative thinking in public policy or in organizational change. It usually takes place in an informal meeting of people who share an interest in finding solutions to a given problem.

The participants in a brainstorming session rapidly trade ideas with the goal of producing a list of possibilities. Ideas are offered and recorded as they are made, with no attempt to criticize or evaluate them. A free discussion of the issues should produce creative thinking and numerous suggestions. It is critical that creativity is encouraged, while no attempt is made to rule out or criticize any proposal at this stage.

After they have generated a long list of ideas the participants then move on to a second step. There they reduce the number of suggestions to come up with a shorter list of alternatives worthy for further consideration.

[Figure 5-3] A Brainstorming Session

Brainstorming can also take the form of written suggestions. Written suggestions may increase the amount of creativity due to anonymity. Some brainstorming variations suggest that creativity is enhanced when some structure is introduced into the discussions.

Brainstorming involves several simple procedures:

- Brainstorming groups should be composed in accordance with the nature of the problem being addressed. This usually means the selection of experts who are particularly knowledgeable about the specific situation.
- The processes of idea generation and idea evaluation should be kept strictly apart. Criticism and debate may inhibit intense group discussion before a broad range of creative ideas have been generated.
- During the step where participants are generating ideas, the meeting atmosphere should be kept as free, non-judgmental, and permissive as possible.
- Participants should move on to evaluate ideas only after they have fully exhausted the process of generating ideas.
- After evaluating the ideas, the group should rank the ideas by their priority and incorporate them into a proposal that contains a conceptualization of the problem along with potential solutions.

Brainstorming is a highly versatile procedure which may involve relatively structured or unstructured activities. This depends on the goals of the procedure and the practical limitations of the situation. Relatively unstructured brainstorming activities are frequent in government agencies and public and private "think tanks."

The main difference between brainstorming and other techniques for problem structuring is that the focus is on groups of knowledgeable experts rather than on individuals. This is particularly effective where groups are heterogeneous, allowing for the creative combination and interplay of ideas that do not usually go together within a discipline. Moreover, brainstorming activities are assessed, not in terms of logical consistency or the plausibility of comparisons, but according to a consensus among the members of brainstorming groups, allowing for a greater collective wisdom to arise from individual ideas.

18 Quick Surveys

Quick surveys involve talking with people in a particular policy network. They may also involve searching through records and documentary sources like hearings transcripts, minutes of meetings, newspapers accounts, and the like for information about a problem and possible policy alternatives.

There are already many people familiar with the issues. They have probably raised many alternatives, and already done a lot of work that may be applicable to the current analysis. Interviewing them, giving them surveys, or reviewing what they have written or said on the issues should produce a short list of possible policy alternatives that have already been given some expert thought. This technique could be particularly useful at the local level where gaining access to the principal policy actors is a real possibility.

19 Literature Reviews

A literature review is a regular tool of students and social scientists. It is a basic standard for peer review. A literature review is an examination of books, journal articles, internet sites, and other sources. The purpose of a literature review is to look for policy alternatives that have been proposed or considered previously. This kind of search could extend to a survey of the options that policy makers have considered or adopted in other policy areas as well. Although peer reviewed literature reviews are rigorous in their scientific method, literature reviews do not need to be comprehensive for policy purposes. Professional and political reviews are less thorough than scientific reviews.

There are many good sources of information for literature reviews. For example, the Korean Environmental Impact Assessment Act required that government agencies conduct an environmental impact analysis, and make it public, before making major decisions such as building highways. Can an impact analysis be applied elsewhere? In other words, why not require that specific studies or reports be conducted and made public prior to reaching a final decision in many other areas of public policy?

Rather than think about abstract ideas, analysts might ask what has worked well in specific real world situations, and therefore what might be considered an effective policy alternative for the present policy. Analysts also want to know which alternatives have been tried elsewhere and did not work well. At least they should have an idea of the pros and cons of various approaches. Analysts can also look to what other nations have tried to do about a particular problem and evaluate their success.

20 Comparison with an Ideal

Sometimes analysts compare policy alternatives with an ideal situation. For example, as part of smart growth planning or sustainability efforts, many communities hold so-called "visioning" meetings in which residents are asked to think about what they want their community to be like in the future. They are asked to think about what kind of residential neighborhoods they want, what kind of downtown should they have, and what kind of recreational opportunities they desire. The goal is to envision an ideal future and use a vision to generate ideas for moving in the desired direction.

Too often in public policy debates, participants assume that an ideal situation is unattainable and therefore not worthy of serious consideration. This is a serious problem. Not attempting the ideal guarantees that it will be never come about. Just by encouraging the expression of an ideal, analysts can at least ensure that practical ideas are evaluated in terms of how close they come to the ideal.

Any of these strategies for generating a list of policy alternatives should help an analyst to think clearly about how to solve a problem. At this point in the process, neither the cost nor the political feasibility of any particular option is the primary concern. Rather, the idea is to think critically about the problem and try to imagine the various ways to address it.

[Box 5-2] ***Men and Women at Work***

What is the ideal pay difference between men and women? Should they receive equal pay?

The *Korea Herald* reported July 1, 2008 that Korea's wage gap between men and women was the largest among countries of the Organization for Economic Cooperation and Development in 2005, according to government data.

The difference was seen as mainly caused by more women being employed in temporary jobs, which pay less than regular jobs, officials said.

Women also earn lower wages because they work for a shorter period than men, as they take time out for childcare, they said. In both cases the cause is the preference in Korea for seniority-based pay over productivity-based pay. Seniority-based systems reward time spent at a job (job tenure) instead of how much work you actually do. Temporary contract employees, who are more often women, spend less time on the job, as do women who leave the workforce temporarily to have children.

Korean women earned an average of 61% of what men earned. This was far below the OECD average of 81%.

The number of male temporary workers was 37% of the total male workforce, while female temporary workers were 58.3% of the total female workforce. Temporary workers refer to employees with contract terms of less than one year.

"Although women are more actively engaged in economic activities, job security for women remains lower than men's," said Sohn Minjung, a researcher at the Samsung Economic Research Institute. The study reported that the nation with the lowest gap was New Zealand, where women received 91% of men's average salary.

Discussion Questions

- What would the ideal Korean economy look like?
- How does this situation compare to your ideal?
- How serious is this problem?
- What can the government do to address this problem?

– Korea Herald

21 The Pool of Policy Alternatives

Constructing alternatives focuses on how to develop the list of alternatives. Specifically, it is the process of gathering options that merit consideration. Learning how to think creatively about public policy is very important, particularly when ineffective policies and programs need to be replaced. How do analysts know which alternatives to consider?

For constructing alternatives the starting point is to see what governments are doing or are able to do. Among their options, governments can regulate, subsidize, ration, tax and spend, contract out, use market incentives, privatize, charge fees for services, educate, create public trust, and commission research. The following discussion summarizes these activities and illustrates them with examples.

Regulate

Regulation is a broad category covering every form of control or direction. It typically includes things like licensing, inspection, enforcement of standards, and application of sanctions (better known as punishments). Government enforces a great variety of environmental, health, workplace safety, and corporate financial regulations.

Subsidize

A subsidy is a form of monetary support that encourages an activity by helping to pay for it. Loans (including student loans), direct payments of benefits, tax credits, price supports, subsidies to farmers, price supports, and low interest loans are all examples of subsidies.

Ration

Rationing means limiting access to scarce resources. When you buy entry tickets to national parks, the government is limiting your access. Limitations are also placed on the coverage of health care services, defining how and to whom benefits are distributed.

Tax and Spend

Taxing an activity at a high-enough level discourages it, while a low tax (or no tax) encourages it. Spending dedicates money to preferred programs. Cigarette taxes discourage smoking. Military spending finances national defense, criminal justice spending pays for prisons and the police, while public education spending pays for teachers and schools.

Contract Out

The government may buy, or contract out for, government

services or products for government agencies from the private sector instead of producing them through the public sector. Contracts for weapons, the purchase of computers and vehicles for government, and food service contracts are all examples of contracting out.

Use Market Incentives

This is a special category of taxation or imposition of fees that creates incentives to change behavior and achieve goals and objectives. Raising gasoline taxes encourages fuel conservation and reduces carbon dioxide emissions without direct government action, allowing the market to encourage consumers to behave in socially-desirable ways. Tax deductions for purchasing auto insurance are another way the government encourages action without compelling it.

Privatize

Privatization represents transferring public services from government to the private sector. This can include turning over management of public services to public corporations(an intermediate form of privatization), as well as proposals for privatizing the national pension system by requiring individuals to manage their own retirement savings.

Charge Fees

Fee for services is a form of "pay as you go" where those who consume a service pay for it. Although not technically a market incentive, charging fees pushes government consumption into the market, forcing a form of rational market rationing. This may include things like public transportation fees, entrance fees to public museums and national parks, as well as port charges.

Educate

The government may provide information to the public through formal programs or other actions. This may include formal public meetings, public education, food safety labels, information on toxic chemicals, appliance energy efficiency labels. The recent decision to mandate that restaurants serving beef post the nation of origin is a form of consumer education.

Create Public Trusts

The government may hold public property indefinitely in trust for citizens. This takes several different forms, such as land conservation trusts, national parks and recreation areas, as well as historical landmarks and national treasures.

Conduct Research

The government may conduct or support research and development. Support for academic studies, defense, medical, and environmental research are all areas where the government is deeply involved in research.

If current policies are not working well enough and a change is needed, analysts might suggest modifying the present policies or trying a different policy approach or strategy.

[Figure 5-4] Providing Information to the Public is an Example of a Government Intervention that is Educational

Present policy could be strengthened. For example, the government could raise standards and penalties for air and water policies. Policy makers could fund programs at a higher level, which might permit improved research, better enforcement, and better public information campaigns. Analysts and policy makers also consider alternatives to conventional regulatory policies, as was done in the United States for many environmental policies during the 1980s and 1990s. This might include a combination of market-based incentives, public information campaigns, and various forms of regulatory reinvention, which are more flexible and efficient policy reforms.

For some policies and agencies policy makers might try different institutional approaches, such as a new way to

[Box 5-3] *Privatization*

According to *Hankyoreh,* the government announced its plans to privatize 50 to 60 of 305 public companies, hoping to raise about ₩63 trillion won. Approximately 258,000 employees would be reduced to about 188,000 through the merger and abolition of about 30 state-run companies.

On May 22, the government announced that it would dispose of its shares in more than fifty public enterprises, including the Korea Development Bank and Woori Bank, as well as its shares in 16 companies that are owned by public firms. The government would dispose of properties, including golf courses, owned by public firms.

In some areas, like ports and airports, management rights would be handed over to the private sector, not the facilities themselves.

Discussion Questions

- What are the arguments for and against privatization?
- Which argument do you prefer?
- Many properties owned by the government compete with private enterprises. Should the government compete with the private sector? Is it better for the government to acquire more enterprises or to get out of such businesses?
- How much should the government focus on providing social goods that only it can provide?
- Does managing enterprises distract from taking care of the public as a whole?

– Hankyoreh Media Company

organize the bureaucracy in charge. For example, the Korean government has had many different ministry reforms where new ministries are founded, some are split off, and others are consolidated and forced together.

Governments are trying another interesting institutional reform option. They make routine government services available online, everything from providing information to tourists to supplying government forms that people can fill out on their computers. Governments report improved efficiency, and users say they are more satisfied with the results and think more highly of agencies than before.

For many policy areas, actions are rooted in one of two views of the problem being confronted, what might be called the supply and demand perspective. If analysts believe a problem such as energy scarcity results from an insufficient supply of energy, they would likely recommend the policy alternative of increasing supply. They would consider actions to boost supplies of energy, whether from fossil fuels(oil, natural gas, and coal), nuclear energy, or alternative energy such as wind or solar power. To consider which policy option will work best or be more efficient or fair, policy makers also have to think about the philosophical and ideological aspects.

22 Policy Design Tools

Policy design refers to the careful consideration, during the policy formulation stage, of the role of government agents and the target population, those who receive benefits or who are the objects of government regulation. For public policies to work, they must be thoroughly based in an understanding of the attitudes and motivations of the policy actors who will decide how the policies are implemented and whether they have the desired effects. If policy actors are rational beings who respond to the incentives and disincentives incorporated into a particular policy. Policy makers should be able to design policies that encourage people to behave in the way that is needed to meet the goals and objectives.

Policy tools are the elements in policy design that cause agents or targets to do something they would not otherwise do with the intention of modifying behavior to solve public problems or attain policy goals. The choice of such tools reflects different views of how people behave and what might lead them to change their behavior.

Policy design is the consideration of a variety of possible approaches, instruments, or tools that may be appropriate for a given policy problem. The tools described here are based on anticipating how different policy actors are likely to respond to what governments attempt to do. There are five policy tools which Schneider and Ingram have distinguished:

- Authority tools
- Inducements and sanctions
- Capacity-building tools
- Hortatory tools
- Learning tools

Authority Tools

They assume people behave because someone in authority asks them to do so. The use of such tools is not always effective or democratic and is dependent on the perceived legitimacy of government. These tools may be particularly suitable during times of crisis when favorable responses by the public are more likely.

Inducements and Sanctions

The assumption is here that people are rational actors who seek to maximize their self interests. Inducements encourage people to act in a certain way because they will gain from doing so. Sanctions are negative incentives or penalties that are thought to discourage behavior that is inconsistent with policy goals.

[Figure 5-5] A Government Proclamation is a Hortatory Tool

Capacity-building Tools

They provide training, education, information, and technical assistance, and they aim to inform or educate and thus empower people, either those in the target population or policy agents.

Hortatory Tools

Governments invoke images and values through speeches, proclamations, and other communications to encourage people to behave in a certain way.

Learning Tools

Policy agents and target populations are encouraged to participate and learn, for example, through citizen advisory panels and collaborative process.

Many public policies are equally dependent on assumptions about how people affected by policy rules will behave. Traffic laws, for example, depend on a driver's willingness to stop at red lights and to keep to the posted speed limit. Additional sanctions may be necessary when people do not respond as expected. Governments impose substantial fines and other penalties for driving under the influence of alcohol as a way of discouraging this behavior. Here the assumption is that a person contemplating a criminal act would adjust his or her behavior with the understanding of the possible punishment.

Discussion Questions

1. What sources of information have you used in your student research?
2. What are the kinds of policy information? How are they related to each other?
3. What is media literacy? How can you easily check information for accuracy? What are some standards for detecting distortion?
4. What is the purpose of a literature review? Where should a policy analyst look in order to conduct one?
5. What kinds of ideals can be the basis for a policy comparison?
6. What government actions do you think are most effective? Why do you think this is true?
7. What government actions can also involve the private sector? Are such actions as useful as government-only action?
8. Give specific examples of each of the policy tools and specify those you think are the most effective.

Vocabulary

academic journal
public opinion survey
policy actor
intuition
statistical analysis
media literacy
policy alternative
policy action
policy outcome
policy performance
reliable information
reliability
information distortion
pertinent information
relevant information
interpretation
brainstorming
consensus

collective wisdom
creativity
idea generation
idea evaluation
policy network
questionnaire
quick surveys
literature reviews
environmental impact
comparison with an ideal
visioning
regulate
license
subsidize
ration
tax and spend
contract out
market incentive
privatize
charge fees
educate
a public trust
reorganization
target population
authority tool
capacity-building tool
hortatory tool
learning tool
inducement
sanction
public information campaign
institutional approach
supply and demand perspective

References

Anderson, James E. (2003). *Public Policymaking,* 5th ed. Houghton Mifflin: Boston, MA.

"Exposing Ex-Minister's Deception Is Child's Play" http://english.chosun.com/w21data/html/news/200806/200806250028.html

"Gender Wage Gap Biggest in OECD" http://www.koreaherald.co.kr/NEWKHSITE/dta/html_dir/2008/07/01/200807010059.asp

Goldenburg, Jacob, Mazursky, David, and Solomon, Sorin (1999). "Creative Sparks" *Science.* September 3:1495-1496.

Kraft, E. Michael, and Furlong, R. Scott (2004). *Public Policy: Politics, Analysis, and Alternatives.* CQ Press: Washington, DC.

Mazmanian, Daniel A., and Kraft, Michael A. (1999). *Toward Sustainable Communities: Transition and Transformations in Environmental Policy.* MIT Press: Cambridge, MA.

Patton, Carl V., and Sawicki, David S. (1993). *Basic Methods of Policy Analysis and Planning,* 2nd ed. Prentice Hall: Englewood Cliffs, NJ.

"The Prosecution's Role as the Government's Strong Arm" http://english.hani.co.kr/arti/english_edition/e_editrial/295927.html.

"Public Companies to be Made Private" http://english.hani.co.kr/arti/english_edition/e_business/289354.html

Schneider, Anne L., and Ingram, Helen (1997). *Policy Design for Democracy* University of Kansas Press: Lawrence, KS.

"The Truth About 'PD Diary" http://english.chosun.com/w21data/html/news/200806/200806260023.html

Vig, Norman J. (2003). "Presidential Leadership and the Environment" in *Environmental Policy,* 5th ed. Edited by Norman J. Vig and Michael A. Kraft. CQ Press: Washington, DC.

WEEK 6 Evaluative Criteria

Summary

A variety of different criteria may be used to evaluate and select alternatives. These criteria include effectiveness, efficiency, equity, ethics, liberty, political feasibility, administrative feasibility, technical feasibility, and social acceptability.

Effectiveness, efficiency, equity, and ethics are four of the most important criteria, as others are generally easier to determine.

Effectiveness is a measure of whether or not or how well the alternative will work.

Efficiency is a comparison of costs and benefits.

Equity is a measure of the fairness of the policy. It is considered in two terms. These are fairness of the process and fairness of the outcome.

Ethics is a measure of whether the policy is right or wrong and of whether it meets moral standards.

Evaluative Criteria

- are the specific dimensions of policy objectives
- can be used to weigh policy options and judge the merits of existing policies or programs
- can also be thought of as justifications or relations for a policy or government action.

Evaluative criteria establish relatively clear standards that can keep policy analysis objective and focused on the issues of greatest concern to the analyst, the intended audience, or the client. Such standards also allow users to rank alternatives

[Figure 6-1] A Couple Evaluating Each Other

Men and women use a variety of evaluative criteria when choosing a partner or spouse. They may rank these in different ways at different times and attach different weights to different criteria in a way that is exactly like the policy analysis process.

in order of their preferences. It makes sense to choose the criteria that fit a given policy area and set of circumstances.

The combination of clear evaluative criteria and careful analysis should make political or administrative feasibility easier to determine whether one policy alternative is better than another.

There are various evaluative criteria. Among these some important criteria are the following that will be discussed:

- Effectiveness
- Efficiency (costs and benefits)
- Equity
- Ethics

The discussion below lists different criteria often used in policy analysis and policy debates. The discussion specifies the meaning of each criterion and the limitations in using it as a standard of judgment. It also indicates the type of public policies for which it is most appropriate. Typically, when these criteria are used, they must be expressed in terms of operational measurements of indicators. For example, analysts usually speak of efficiency in terms of monetary costs in relation to the value of benefits expected to be realized from a government action, such as improved food safety. Effectiveness can be measured in terms of the likelihood of reaching a specific policy objective, such as reducing auto accident rates by twenty percent over a five-year period.

Effectiveness

This is the likelihood of achieving the policy's goals and

objectives or a demonstrated achievement of them. The difficulty in estimating effectiveness lies in that estimates involve an uncertain projection of future events. Virtually all policy proposals that consider how well government programs work use effectiveness as a criterion.

Efficiency

This represents the achievement of program goals or benefits at an acceptable cost. It is considered through looking at benefits in relationship to the costs. It may be seen as the least cost for a given benefit or the largest benefit for a given cost. Measuring all the costs and benefits is not always possible. Furthermore, policy decision making reflects political choices as much as efficiency. Regulatory policies, such as workplace safety and environmental protection and any consideration of market-based approaches all use efficiency.

Equity

Equity represents fairness or justice in the distribution of the policy's costs, benefits, and risks across population subgroups. There are difficulties in finding techniques to measure equity. There is also disagreement over whether equity means a fair process (procedural equity) or equal outcomes (distributive equity).

Disability rights, tax equity, access to health services and higher education all include assessments of equity.

Liberty/Freedom

This is the extent to which public policy extends or restricts privacy and individual rights and choices. Assessments of impacts on freedom are often clouded by ideological beliefs about the role of government, however. These considerations are raised in restrictions on internet use, property rights, abortion rights, and regulatory actions that constrain choices of corporations and individuals.

Political Feasibility

This is the extent to which elected officials accept and support a policy proposal. There is no set formula, making it difficult to determine. It depends on perceptions of the issues and on changing economic and political conditions. Any controversial policy, such as changes in environmental regulations or symbolic issues in relations with the US and Japan, needs to be considered in terms of political feasibility.

Social Acceptability

This is the extent to which the public will accept and support a policy proposal. It is difficult to determine even when public support can be measured. It depends on the saliency of the issues and the level of public awareness. Any controversial policy, such as importing American beef, changing the administrative capitol, or building a national canal, must take social acceptability into consideration.

Administrative Feasibility

This is the likelihood that a department or agency can implement the policy well. It involves a projection of available resources and agency behavior that can be difficult to estimate. Expansion of agency duties, the use of new policy approaches or new technologies, and policies with complicated institutional structures often raise questions of administrative feasibility.

Technical Feasibility

This final criterion is the availability and reliability of the technology needed for policy implementation. It is often difficult to anticipate technological change that could alter feasibility. Science and technology policy, environmental and energy policies, telecommunications, and defense policies often raise technological and technical feasibility concerns.

23 Effectiveness

Effectiveness, how well a policy is working, is a nearly universal concern. Analysts and policymakers speak of what works and what does not work, about policy success and the lack of it. In a narrow sense, effectiveness refers to reaching the stated goals and objectives of a policy or policy action. For a program already in existence, evaluation of its effectiveness usually depends on whether it has achieved the expected results or policy outcomes.

For example, are environmental policies improving air quality? Have public school students mastered necessary learning outcomes? Assessments like these require that analysts develop suitable indicators or measurements for the specified outcomes. For a proposed policy, they try to estimate the likelihood that such goals and objectives would be attained if the proposal is adopted. This view of effectiveness is rather narrow, however, because programs usually have multiple goals and objectives and may succeed at some and fall short on others. Moreover, some objectives may be attainable only over a long period of time. This makes assessment of short-term outcomes problematic. Another limitation is that estimating the probability that a proposal will be effective, or more effective than the present policy, requires a forecast of future conditions and events. This is always an uncertain activity. In addition, analysts must learn to deal with a political environment in which politicians often exaggerate the weaknesses of current programs and tout the strengths of alternatives based more on ideological beliefs than any assessment of empirical evidence of program effectiveness.

24 Costs, Benefits, and Efficiency

Policy effectiveness is a nearly universally accepted standard in contemporary policymaking. The interest in keeping the cost of government programs within reason is also universal. Whether efficiency is a specific measurement of costs in relation to benefits or gaining the most benefits for a fixed cost the criterion amounts to the same thing. It strongly encourages analysts to think about the overall costs and benefits of existing programs and the various proposals to change them or substitute something different. However, calculating societal benefits and costs is not easy, particularly when they must be expressed in monetary terms.

For example, how do analysts calculate the national security benefits of basing American soldiers in Korea compared to the military costs or to the inevitable property damages and injuries to innocent civilians (see Box 8-1)? Should a nation simply do whatever it takes to provide for security and accept the costs?

[Box 6-1] *The Cost of Moving from Yongsan*

Korea will have to pay more than ₩8.9 trillion to relocate US bases to Pyeongtaek, Gyeonggi, *Chosun Ilbo* reported June 9, 2008.

The costs Korea was supposed to bear were originally estimated at ₩5.59 trillion, but are likely to increase by another ₩3.3 trillion. This includes ₩1 trillion in direct costs and ₩2.3 trillion in indirect costs.

The delayed construction of the Pyeongtaek base has caused conflict between Korea and the US, which is insisting on completion by 2012.

The added costs include special subsidies for Pyeongtaek, costs for environmental restoration of old US bases, and additional construction costs were added. A new forecast of the project added an additional ₩1 trillion in construction costs. The Defense Ministry had planned to raise the ₩1 trillion through its general accounts and ₩4.7 trillion from the sale of US bases. However, according to the audit, the estimated amount totalling ₩6.3 trillion is still ₩2.6 trillion" short from what is actually needed, even if these two amounts are added by ₩611 billion the ministry has already earmarked.

The ministry's report said, "A special measure to push for a smooth implementation of the project, as it is currently estimated that we will be short ₩2.6 trillion, is necessary. A senior Defense Ministry official said, "The exact construction costs and period will be announced after consultations with the US based on the outcome of the PMC's review after August."

Discussion Questions

- The sale of properties recovered from the US military will not come close to compensating for the costs. Is the move still justified?
- What other benefits can be included to justify the costs of the move?
- What intangible benefits does the move confer?
- What are some alternative policies that would better benefit costs and benefits?

– Chosun Ilbo

Defenders of the efficiency criterion assume that the benefits and costs are more or less equally distributed among the population. The benefits of policies such as agricultural subsidies or subsidized tuition for college students go to particular groups in the population, but all taxpayers bear the costs. For regulatory policies, such as controls on polluting power plants, the larger society receives the benefits, but the owners of the plant and the stakeholders bear the costs. Analysts therefore need to inquire into the distribution of benefits and costs as part of any attempt to examine economic efficiency and its acceptability.

Efficiency is a way of justifying government action on the basis of economic concepts. Sometimes efficiency is expressed in terms of the relative virtues of government intervention and the operation of the free market in promoting social welfare.

25 Equity

Equity has at least two different meanings in contemporary policy debates:

- Process equity
- Outcomes (end-result) equity

Process equity

This type of equity refers to the decision-making process. If it is voluntary, open, and fair to all participants, then analysts and citizens are more likely to judge the results to be equitable even if some people ultimately have better outcomes than others by gaining more benefits such as higher education, better jobs, greater income, and nicer apartments. Those who hold these views tend to believe strongly in the rights of individuals and the freedom to use and dispose of their resources as they see fit. They resist government efforts to promote equality beyond assuring equal opportunity to participate in the nation's decisions. Political conservatives are more likely to be concerned with process equity.

Outcomes equity

Outcomes equity or fairness refers to just outcomes or the fair distribution of societal goods such as wealth, income, or political power. This is because political institutions and social structures, such as sexism and regionalism and other forms of discrimination affect the achievement of such goods. The acquisition of societal goods is not solely a function of the individual qualities of ambition, talent, and a strong work ethic. People who hold this view are more likely than others to favor government intervention to promote the equitable distribution of society's resources. Political liberals are likely to identify with the concept of outcomes equity.

Equity criteria are likely to be central to any consideration of redistributive policies, such as tax reform, social welfare, efforts to enhance access to education or health services, and assistance to the poor. Policy analysts might want to ask who receives the benefits of policy action, who does not, and who pays for the costs of the program. In this context, the relevant actors are not usually individuals, but rather groups of people. They can be the wealthy, the middle class, or the poor. They may be divided between city dwellers, suburbanites, and rural residents. Ordinary people may be pitted against huge corporations. Equity issues are pervasive in policy disputes, from tax reform proposals to actions that might restrict access to higher education, such as raising tuition.

26 Ethics

Ethics are a fundamental consideration that must be considered in policy evaluation. Ethics do not simply apply to an analyst's preferences but are obligatory criteria of political judgment. Some people argue that it is unnecessary for policy analysts to include ethics or values in their work because they think ethics and normative values are not part of rational analysis. Alternately, they may believe that analysts are incapable of objective analysis because they inevitably inject their personal biases into any such assessment. Explicit analysis of ethics and values could greatly enhance the quality of argument and debate in policymaking bodies.

It is easier for analysts to stress criteria such as effectiveness and efficiency where an assessment can be based on hard data such as measurable costs and benefits. Normative issues deserve serious consideration. Analysis that ignores basic issues such as the role of government authority, individual rights, or the public interest is incomplete and inadequate.

Policy debates over privacy, property rights, copyright laws, research on human stem cells derived from embryos, and many other contemporary issues clearly require an assessment in terms of normative and legal criteria, not just economics. Even for a seemingly technical subject such on as nuclear waste disposal, it is both possible and necessary to analyze the ethical issues of the effect on future generations, voluntarism in the selection of sites for waste repositories, public involvement in decision making, and fairness to host communities in terms of benefits that can be provided.

There are many different bases of evaluative criteria on which to analyze policy. Students of public policy need to be aware of the range of standards that are applied and be alert to their strengths and limits and the tradeoffs between them. For example, promoting the public's welfare through food safety or environmental protection policies imposes a cost on individuals and corporations. Restrictions on their freedom or liberty may be justified by the public's gain. Conversely, at times, the protection of individual rights and liberties is so important that society is willing to tolerate activity that many find abhorrent. Regime values, the values of the society and the government in question, are a useful set of ethical standards.

Policy makers and analysts want policy action to be effective, but they also want to minimize costs, or to promote the most equitable solution, or to maintain individual rights. It is a rare policy action that can maximize each of these criteria simultaneously. The analysts must therefore figure out which criteria are most important to the public or a client for the analysis and use those preferences to rank policy alternatives from best to worse. The multiple criteria can be used at the same time to assess the attractiveness of different policy options.

Discussion Questions

1. What do analysts need to determine evaluative criteria?
2. What are the best evaluative criteria? What are their strengths and weaknesses?
3. How are efficiency and effectiveness different?
4. What are the contradictions between the two equity standards? How can they be kept in balance?
5. What ethical standards should be used when judging policy?

Vocabulary

evaluative criteria
effectiveness
efficiency
costs and benefits
equity
outcome equity
process equity
ethics
regime values
liberty
political feasibility
administrative feasibility
operational measurement
technical feasibility
redistributive policy
regime value
social acceptability
societal benefit

References

Amy, Douglas J. (1984). "Why Policy Analysis and Ethics are Incompatible" *Journal of Policy analysis and Management.* 3: 573-591.

Anderson, Charles W. (1979). "The Place of Principles in Policy Analysis" *American Political Science Review.* 73: 711-723.

Dunn, N. William (1994). *Public Policy Analysis: An Introduction.* Prentice-Hall: Englewood Cliffs, NJ.

Freeman, A. Myrick III (2000). "Economics, Incentives, and Environmental Regulation" in *Environmental Policy,* 4th ed. Edited by Norman J. Vig and Michael E. Kraft. CQ Press: Washington, DC.

Kraft, Michael E. (2000). "Policy Design and the Acceptability of Environmental Risks: Nuclear Waste Disposal in Canada and the United States" *Policy Studies Journal.* 28 (1): 206-218.

Kraft, E. Michael, and Furlong, R. Scott (2004). *Public Policy: Politics, Analysis, and Alternatives.* CQ Press: Washington, DC.

Sabatier, Paul A., Jenkins-Smith, Hank C., eds. (1993). *Policy Change and Learning: An Advocacy Coalition Approach* Westview Press: Boulder, CO.

Stone, Deborah (2002). *Policy Paradox: The Art of Political Decisionmaking.* W.W. Norton: New York, NY.

"U.S. Base Move to Cost More Than W8.9 Trillion" http://english.chosun.com/w21data/html/news/200806/200806090008.html

Weimer, L. David, and Vining, R. Aidan (2005). *Policy Analysis: Concepts and Practice.* Pearson Prentice Hall: Englewood Cliffs, NJ.

Weiss, Carol H. (1992). *Organizations for Policy Analysis: Helping Government Think.* Sage: Newbury Park, CA.

Whiteman, David (1995). *Communication in Congress: Members, Staff, and the Search for Information.* University of Kansas Press: Lawrence, KS.

WEEK 7 Cost－Benefit Analysis(CBA) Ⅰ

Summary

Cost-benefit analysis(CBA) is a common policy analysis tool that focuses on policy efficiency. It is usually employed before investment with estimates of projected costs and benefits, although it may also be used after investment to evaluate a program using actual costs and benefits.

CBA consists of five elements. These are objectives, alternatives, costs, a model, and a criterion.

CBA takes place in five steps. The first step is establishing alternatives. The next step is to identify all affected parties along with the costs and benefits that will impact them. Step three is to estimate or measure all of the benefits and costs. After that, all benefits and costs need to be given a monetary value. For comparison across different time periods, all values should be calculated and compared for all of the alternatives, with the most desirable one chosen on the basis of the evaluative criterion.

Benefits and costs may be real, pecuniary, direct, indirect, internal, and external.

There are many difficulties in measuring costs and benefits.

The mathématical calculations always include various assumptions and judgments, including the choice of rates for calculating discount to present value. Uncertainty is a major area for making judgments.

There are varieties in methods of policy analysis. The leading methods of policy analysis draw heavily from economics and focus on the evaluative criterion of efficiency, particularly for cost-benefit and cost effectiveness analyses. The methods are tools for critical thinking about public policy.

27 What does CBA Mean?

Cost-benefit analysis is directed toward all resource allocation decisions. It is used to address the question of whether a public program or project should be undertaken and at what level such programs and projects should be supported. It is a tool designed to evaluate the feasibility of specific projects, to select preferred projects from a range of possible projects, and to justify projects in the budgetary process. Formal cost-benefit models are most typically used in pre-investment analysis based on before-the-fact estimates of costs and benefits. It is also used most frequently in evaluating the worthiness of proposed infrastructure improvements or research and development projects. It has been applied much more to capital investment problems than to operating program decisions.

CBA was initially developed in water resources management. It was applied to projects designed to improve navigation, irrigation, and flood control, and to provide hydroelectric power, water supply, and recreational facilities. It has also been widely used in the field of transportation and more recently has been extended to urban renewal and human resource program areas, including education and health.

28 CBA Models

The general principle underlying CBA is quite simple. Add up the monetary values of all the benefits to be derived from a project and all the costs to be incurred by the project, and compare them. In general, if the total amount of benefits exceeds total costs, the project is justified and should be undertaken or included in the pool of alternatives from which one project will be selected. CBA consists of five elements: 1) objectives, 2) alternatives, 3) costs, 4) a model, and 5) a criterion. In cost-benefit applications there must be no ambiguity about objectives because the identification and measurement of benefits are derived from program objectives.

Benefits are outcomes that move toward specified objectives, the achievement of intended impacts. They may represent change from present conditions or the maintenance of conditions that would be expected to deteriorate if the program or project were not implemented.

The alternatives represent competing possible uses of resources. They may consist of one individual program or project versus no public project (where the alternative is to leave the resources in the private sector and not undertake such a project) or a number of specified projects differing in terms of purpose, scope, location, size, or design characteristics.

Regardless, the alternatives must be described in sufficient detail to differentiate among their anticipated costs and benefits.

[Figure 7-1] CBA is like Comparing Income and Expenses

날짜 (내역)	수 입	날짜 (내역)	지 출
07년 12/10 첫모임 기금	1,320,000	07년 12/10 경복궁 식대	303,000
12/10 배광준	1,000,000	12/10 간판	100,000
12/17 김이형	1,000,000	12/10 사무실 수리비	200,000
12/18 사무실 오픈 때	460,000	12/10 통장도장	20,000
12/19 배철수	1,000,000	12/11 난로구입비	95,500
12/23 박철호	100,000	12/12 책상 구입 및 수리비	466,000
1/2 배광준	4,000,000	12/12 연탄대금	105,000
1/2 오경옥(정채철)	5,000,000	12/18 사무실 오픈때	252,650
1/8 최종수	500,000	12/18 등기우편 대금	318,450
1/8 배철수	4,000,000	12/18 인쇄물 대금	35,000
1/19 권병윤	500,000	12/18 현수막 제작비	250,000
2/4 배광준	3,000,000	12/24 등기우편 대금	4,100
2/4 정재철	3,000,000	1/3 인쇄물비	107,330
2/4 배철수	3,000,000	1/7 변호사비	10,000,000
12월 결산이자	17	1/11 인쇄물비	49,580
		1/14 이재희	500,000
		1/25 하나로텔레콤	52,906
		2/4 변호사비	11,000,000
		2/25 하나로텔레콤	36,102
		2/28 사무실 전화요금	177,190
합 계	27880017	합 계	23,569,808

An accountant calculates profit and loss by adding up all of the expenses and all of the income and compares them. Likewise, the analyst adds up the monetary values of all the benefits of a project and compares them to all of the costs to be incurred by the project.

[Box 7-1] **Koreans not Good at Korean?**

The proficiency of Koreans in their mother tongue has declined in recent years as many take Korean-language education for granted.

Chosun Ilbo reported on July 3, 2008 about a nationwide study of the results of tests of middle school students between 2004 and 2006. Those receiving good or excellent marks in Korean fell from 14.1% in 2004 to 11% in 2006. On the other hand, those who received good or excellent grades in English rose from 18.6% to 20.5%.

In 2001, the Korean Education Development Institute released a report on Koreans' reading comprehension and compared it with that of other OECD countries. Koreans adults scored 237.5 out of 500 points when tested on their ability to understand, ranking 18th out of 22. Sweden came first with 305.6 points. Korea was also in the middle to lower ranks in comprehending newspaper editorials, poems and novels.

A JobKorea survey of 330 human resources managers in Korean firms revealed that 59.7% were unhappy with the level of Korean proficiency of new employees, with 49.4% saying they were "dissatisfied" and 10.3% "very dissatisfied."

Experts say neglect of Chinese characters education in the school curriculum is one of the major reasons for this decline. They claim the study of Chinese characters is essential as 70% of Korean vocabulary is made of Chinese characters. Prof. Lee Jongmook of the Department of Korean Language and Literature at Seoul National University said, "The fundamental remedy would be to strengthen the study of Chinese characters in the school curriculum, and to help children develop reading skills by studying the classics from adolescence."

Lack of time committed to reading also contributes to dwindling Korean proficiency. According to statistics on Koreans' reading habits released by the Ministry of Culture, Sports and Tourism last year, adults managed to read only one book per month, and one in four did not read books at all.

Discussion Questions

- How serious is the problem cited in the study?
- How do you explain the decline in Korean language proficiency noted in the study?
- How can this issue be addressed?
- Many people assume that there is a trade-off between learning two languages. Psycholinguists, however, find that properly learning a second language generally improves ability in the first language. Do you think Koreans study English at the expense of Korean?
- What are the costs and benefits of English language education in Korea?

– Chosun Ilbo

Costs represent forgone benefits of some kind. These include resources that are directly consumed by the project (budget costs) and thus not available for alternative uses, and secondary costs that are imposed by the project's undertaking. These secondary costs usually represent existing benefits of some sort that are reduced or eliminated by virtue of undertaking the project. Benefits and costs are really two sides of the same coin, in that costs can be evaluated only in terms of forgone benefits.

29 Purpose and Procedural Overview of CBA

The purpose of a cost-benefit model is to develop the structural relationships between characteristics of the alternatives and their impacts in order to trace through the anticipated costs and benefits of each of the alternatives. This model building is the real core of the analysis and is the stage that exerts the heavy demands on evaluation research as mentioned above. The validity of the cost and benefit estimates generated by the model is only as sound as the existing knowledge of the relevant causal relationships on which the model is based. Finally, the criterion is the basis upon which the preferred alternative will be determined. For example, it might be to select that project that has the highest ratio of total benefits to total costs.

Procedural Overview

The application of a cost-benefit analysis proceeds in five steps:

- Establish the alternatives. Although the analyst often takes the alternatives as already given, setting the scope of the choice set in the first place is a critical element in CBA. Public projects are characterized by the high degree of interdependencies, incompatibilities, and trade-offs made necessary by budget constraints. As a result, care must be taken to develop a set of alternative choices with common constraints. Inter-project consequences should also be taken into account. An important criticism of practical applications of the technique is that sophisticated models are commonly applied to alternatives that are chosen haphazardly in the first place.

- Identify all affected parties and the types of benefits and costs expected to result from the alternatives.
- Given the types of benefits and costs, develop separately for each alternative measure or estimate the extent to which each type of impact will occur. While Step 2 is conceptual in nature, Step 3 is highly analytical.
- Evaluate these varying amounts of different types of costs and benefits in monetary terms. The monetary values of costs and benefits expected to occur at different points in time must then be discounted to their present value.
- Finally, compare the alternatives in terms of the present value of their benefits and costs, selecting the most desirable alternative based on some previously determined criterion.

The most difficult steps for the analyst are two through four, particularly steps three and four. These are very sensitive to the particular design characteristics of the alternatives. They also need to consider the context into which the program or project is to be introduced. They remain heavily dependent on the general state of knowledge in the subject area. Steps three and four often constitute great challenges for valid measurement. This is really the basic problem facing analysts.

An example of comparing costs and benefits is that the government is considering increasing the cost of bus fare. One option is to increase it by ₩400. There is public complaint and a second option is considered to increase it by only ₩300. The increased price of a bus trip therefore would fall from ₩400 per passenger kilometer to ₩300. The quantity demanded is expected to increase from 120 million passenger kilometers per year to 135 million.

The consumers' surplus between the two options is calculated at approximately ₩12.75 billion per year if the ₩300 option is chosen. These are the relative benefits of the option.

The relative financial cost to the bus company of the ₩300 is ₩9.85 billion per year.

₩12.75 billion − ₩9.85 billion = ₩2.9 billion

The benefit to bus users exceeds the financial cost to the bus company by ₩2.9 billion. Choosing the ₩300 increase option would deliver a net social benefit of ₩2.9 billion to society.

30 Classes of Benefits and Costs

A major strength of CBA in theory is that it provides a comprehensive framework for incorporating all costs and benefits in the analysis, including externalities. However, this same strength presents corresponding dangers to the practical application of the method. A major difficulty is ascertaining "when to stop counting and what not to count."

Real versus Pecuniary

There are many classes of benefits and costs, the foremost distinction being that between real benefits and costs as opposed to pecuniary impacts.

Real benefits and costs represent changes in society's satisfaction derived from production and consumption. Real benefits reflect an addition to the welfare of the community or society as a whole, while real costs represent an actual decrease in this overall welfare or the loss of an opportunity to increase society's welfare in some manner.

Costs and benefits do not reflect gains or losses to the society as a whole, but rather gains to some individuals or groups that are offset by losses incurred by others. Pecuniary effects are attributable to changes in relative prices brought about by the introduction of new facilities or services. They do not affect the overall cost-benefit ration of a proposal, but they are relevant in assessing distributional consequences. If all costs and benefits to all affected parties are listed, pecuniary items will appear twice and cancel out one another.

Direct versus Indirect

Real costs and benefits can be further classified in a number of ways, in particular according to the distinction between direct (primary) versus indirect (secondary) benefits and costs. It has been pointed out that it is incorrect to talk about secondary benefits that should be excluded from the analysis because there are no such things. Rather, indirect or secondary impacts are benefits and costs in relation to secondary, perhaps non-efficiency oriented, objectives.

Direct costs are those incurred to establish and operate a program or to build a facility including one-time fixed costs, investment costs, and recurring costs. They have been itemized as follows.

- One-time fixed costs:
  Research

Planning
Test and evaluation

- Investment costs:
  Land
  Building and facilities
  Equipment and vehicles
  Initial training

- Recurring costs (operating and maintenance costs):

Personnel salaries wages, and fringe benefits for direct operations

Maintenance of equipment, vehicles, and buildings

Replacement and recurring training costs

Direct contributions and payments to citizens, welfare such as payments to the needy

Payments to extra-governmental institutions for services for citizens, e.g., payments to agencies for foster home services

Miscellaneous support (overhead) costs

A comprehensive cost-benefit analysis incorporates all direct costs plus indirect costs, all third party costs and negative impacts of the program.

Tangible benefits and costs are those that may seem to be more economic in nature because they can be valued in the marketplace. Intangible benefits and costs may be no less important than tangible impacts, but they are often much more difficult to evaluate in monetary terms because they are not priced in the marketplace.

Inside versus Outside

Inside costs and benefits occur within the jurisdiction for which the cost-benefit analysis is being performed, whereas outside costs and benefits relate to jurisdictions other than that which is undertaking the project. For example, a dam and reservoir built upstream might reduce the threat of flooding in another jurisdiction downstream. This would be a real outside benefit.

The government is considering constructing a highway bypass. The benefits and costs are calculated and listed below in Table 7-1.

[Table 7-1] Benefits and Costs Balance Sheet for Highway Bypass Construction

Benefits	Costs
Toll revenue: ₩200,000,000	Land and leveled structures: ₩150,000,000
Time saved: ₩550,000,000	Materials and overhead: ₩100,000,000
Decreased congestion: ₩150,000,000	Labor: ₩300,000,000
Reduction of pollution: ₩110,000,000	Engineering and geological surveys: ₩50,000,000
Fewer accidents: ₩1,500,000,000	Operating and maintenance: ₩300,000,000
Faster buses and deliveries: ₩50,000,000	Residential property values in the vicinity: ₩75,000,000
	Local bond interest: ₩75,000,000

The benefits will include a toll charged at the bypass, generating revenue, time savings, decreased congestion, fewer accidents, faster bus travel and commercial deliveries.

As an example of how these benefits are calculated, the benefit of fewer accidents assumes there are 50 accidents caused by the lack of a bypass. Therefore there will be 50 fewer accidents a year. The average cost of these accidents is ₩3,000,000 per accident. The figure of ₩1,500,000,000 = 50 accidents x ₩3,000,000/accident.

For faster bus and commercial delivery trips, the assumption is 10,000 trips a year with 10 minutes saved per trip with an average value of travel time of ₩50 per minute.

10,000 trips x ₩500/trip x 10 minutes/trip = ₩50,000,000

The costs include the construction costs of land, materials, and labor. Other costs include engineering, geological surveys, operations and maintenance, decrease in property values close to the bypass, and the cost of interest on a bond issue to finance the project.

The benefits and costs are compared through the formula:

net benefits = total benefits − total costs

total benefits = ₩200,000,000 + ₩550,000,000 + ₩150,000,000 + ₩110,000,000 + ₩1,500,000,000 + ₩50,000,000 = ₩2,560,000,000

total costs = ₩150,000,000 + ₩100,000,000 + ₩300,000,000 + ₩50,000,000 + ₩300,000,000 + ₩75,000,000 + ₩75,000,000 = ₩1,050,000,000

net benefits = ₩2,560,000,000 − ₩1,050,000,000 = ₩1,510,000,000

benefit-cost ratio = benefit ÷ cost =

₩2,560,000,000/₩1,050,000,000 = 2.438

31 Measuring Costs and Benefits

Given the identification of the various kinds of costs and benefits to be considered, the more challenging aspect of model development involves estimating how much of each class of impact should be anticipated and affixing monetary values to them. The final output of the formal model is the present monetary value of all benefits and all costs, or the net worth of the project at present. This entails making two sets of monetary valuations, pertaining to 1) the value of costs and benefits at the time they occur, and 2) their value discounted to the present.

A whole host of measurement problems arises in moving to this point. Many of these problems stem from uncertainty surrounding future impacts. The cost-benefit analyst is plagued by uncertainties about what all the costs and benefits will be and extent to which they will materialize in future years, as well as uncertainties about the monetary value of these impacts and the appropriate rate for discounting them to their present value. Dealing with these uncertainties begs the very question that benefit-cost analysis is intended to address: What are the advantages and disadvantages of a given proposal?

A second type of problem is that some classes of costs and benefits do not lend themselves very well to monetary valuation or quantitative measurement in any units. For example, it is very difficult to incorporate esthetics or psychological values in cost-benefit accounts. Benefit-cost analysis attempts to quantify all the relevant factors in a common denominator, money, but this often must be supplemented with qualitative analysis. When qualitative aspects are ignored, secondary impacts and intangibles are most likely to be excluded, and this can bias the conclusions tremendously. The more costs and benefits that must be excluded from the formal model, the more important it is to complement the model with qualitative analysis. If these qualitative factors are judged not to vary much among the alternatives, however, this task is greatly simplified.

Although direct costs are usually considered to be the easiest effects to measure, even these factors often prove elusive. They may be open to widely differing interpretations.

As an example of the difficulties in operationalizing a complete benefit-cost analysis is a "soft" program area, consider the comparison of four alternative employment and training activities of the American federal government shown in Table 7-2.

[Table 7-2] Costs and Benefits of Employment and Training Programs

Alternative Policy Options	Current fiscal year cost per participant (dollars)	Potential future increases in annual earnings (dollars)
Skill development	1,600-1,900	400-800
Job development (direct employment creation)	4,700-5,800	300-700
Employability development	2,600-3,500	200-400
Work experience (direct part-time employment creation)	500-2,300	0-200

The cost estimates are based on direct expenditures only, shown for one fiscal year, whereas the projected benefits are limited to an estimate of the annual increases in earnings by program participants. On this basis, the skill development strategies would seem to be the most successful. However, it must be noted that a number of relevant benefits and costs are not included because they are difficult to quantify. These include reductions in the administrative costs of income maintenance programs and the foregone earnings during training of participants in those programs. For the work experience programs, immediate income assistance would be an important benefit as well. Even in terms of future increases in earnings, a lack of information on the persistence in annual earnings gains prevents an estimate of the total value of this direct benefit. The figures in the table consider only the years immediately after participation in these programs. Furthermore, a complete analysis would have to include many more types of benefits and costs to the participants, taxpayers, and society at large.

Discount Rates

A crucial step in calculating benefits and costs is the discounting of all monetary values to their present worth. This is necessary because the value of a particular benefit or cost depends on when it will occur. Future benefits are less valuable than present benefits. A thousand won now is worth more than a thousand won a year from now because presumably it can be invested and generate a greater total value. For example, ₩1,000 today can be invested and will be worth ₩1,040-₩1,100 in a year. Therefore we cannot say that ₩1,000 today equals ₩1,000 in a year.

The further into the future a given cost or benefit is expected to occur, the lower its present value. Most projects generate different flows in the levels of costs and benefits across time.

The only fair basis for evaluating the relationship of benefits to costs is to discount both cost and benefit streams to their present value. For example, many investments in human resource program areas such as health and education have heavy costs early in the project, while the benefits accrue slowly at first, then rise rapidly and level off. Comparing undiscounted benefits and costs would overstate the desirability of the project.

In general, there is a great controversy over the way in which future benefits and costs should be discounted, and with respect to any given project there may be much uncertainty about the proper discount rate to be applied. The continuing debate among economists over appropriate discount rates depends heavily on values. Those favoring an expansion of the public sector justify a high discount rate. The issue is critical because what is at stake is the allocation of resources between the public and private sectors.

Discount rates used by the national government generally range from 3% to 15%, and the time span may easily extend to 50 years or more. The rate actually employed in a given analysis is critical because the benefit-cost ratio may turn out to be greater or less than one, depending on the discount rate alone. For example, there was a study by the US General Accounting Office on the cost-effectiveness of the purchase versus leasing of a fleet of tankers. The study determined that a discount rate of 6% called for the US Navy to purchase the tankers, but that at a 10% discount rate leasing would be the preferred alternative.

The problem of which discount rate is appropriate involves many complex macroeconomic considerations. These include the rate of private saving, government policy regarding economic growth, and benefit trade-offs between present and future generations. In terms of economic principles there is no correct discount rate. The selection of a rate to be applied in a particular analysis may be highly judgmental. Analysts should be aware that changing the rate may be an easy way to make a program look more or less attractive. Therefore this decision needs to be across a range of values, follow standard procedures, or be very well justified.

Private Rates

Either private rates or social rates may be employed. Private discount rates represent interest rates, the cost of borrowing money, in the private sector. It is often held that these are appropriate because in a perfectly competitive market the prevailing private rate represents the time preference of individuals and households making marginal valuations between savings and consumption. Moreover, it is argued that because the private sector is the source of funds for public investment, the private rate is appropriate for discounting the benefits of public projects because it measures the benefits that will accrue if the funds are left in the private sector.

One problem with using the private rate is that there are many private rates. Problems with the use of private rates also include that they do not reflect the full range of external costs incurred by private investment, and there is a discrepancy, occasioned by taxes on income, between the gross rate of return and the after-tax rate of return. In addition, it has been argued that private interest rates are inappropriate for discounting public sector investment because they are based in part on the risk of loss involved in making private loans. Loans to governments are largely risk free so private rates have been considered too high for discounting the costs and benefits of public projects. The point here is that in acknowledging risk, investors will require a higher interest rate than the return they actually expect to receive from all their investments in the long run, thereby overstating the discounting of future yields to present values.

Social Rates

Many critics of the use of private rates advocate that the discount rate may be set lower than private rates as an instrument of public policy to correct for private households that fail to see the importance of saving, investment, and future consumption. The theory underlying such a social time preference rate is based on the notion of delayed rewards and a concern for the welfare of future generations. Reduced consumption and increased investment will produce greater future benefits. Furthermore, using a lower, social discount rate may be more appropriate in terms of undertaking public projects aimed at guaranteeing a clean, healthy physical environment for future generations. In addition, advocates of a social rate point out that social time preference is not simply an aggregation of individual time preferences, because individuals may be better off undertaking more investment collectively than by undertaking the sum of investments they would find it desirable to make privately.

Clearly, there are problems in applying social rates of discount, too. Operationally there is no obvious social time preference rate to select, and theoretically there is a problem relating to whether the sources to be withdrawn from the private sector would be diverted from consumption or investment.

The whole notion of setting a social rate to correct for deficiencies of the private rate is in direct contrast to the principle of citizen/consumer sovereignty. This is the principle on which the philosophy of benefit-cost analysis is based.

Furthermore, it is not really clear the social rate would be lower than the prevailing private rate. Individuals do not foresee the rise in income due to technological progress so they overestimate the value of consumption derived from present savings. Therefore, to correct for this the proper social rate should be greater than the private rate. In many underdeveloped nations, policies of deficit financing of economic development already overstate the value of future benefits as compared with present consumer preferences.

Practical Approaches

The most common approach is not to base the discounting of the benefit stream on the prevailing rate of return in the private sector or on an estimate of the social time preference, but rather on the government's cost of borrowing funds.

The long term borrowing rate is usually considered appropriate. A variation used by some governments is to adjust this rate upward to allow for the loss of tax revenue that results from the decrease in private sector activity. The present value of benefits is compared to actual project costs. Similarly, it has been advocated that governments use the rates at which they can borrow money even though there is wide variation in these rates among regions and units of government, because the problem facing them is the efficient allocation of resources within their region. In part, this convention is based on a financial, rather than economic, justification. In the face of difficulties in determining discount rates based on real opportunity costs, government should undertake projects up to the point beyond which its money outlay is not expected to be recovered.

Given a lack of confidence that a comparison of benefits and costs based on one assumed discount rate is valid, the analysts may prefer to treat the appropriate discount rate as an uncertainty and evaluate costs and benefits using a range of reasonable rates. This can be used to indicate how sensitive the results are to the assumption of a discount rate and the ranges within which different alternatives are preferred. Finally, an alternative to the assumption of a discount rate is the internal rate of return method.

Computing Present Value

The present value of a future benefit or cost is computed by applying a discount factor to the future monetary value in question. The discount factor can be computed, given a discount rate and the number of years over which the future monetary values is to be discounted.

When cost and benefits streams are uneven, that is when the monetary values vary from year to year over the time span involved, each future year benefit and cost must be discounted separately to present value. The formula for the discount factor for a single future monetary value is:

$$1/(1+r)^n$$

r denotes the discount rate and n stands for the number of

years by which the monetary value is to be discounted.

The discount factor for computing the present value of a ₩230,000,000 future benefit to be discounted by a 10% discount rate over five years is shown to be 0.611. This can be interpreted as the present value of ₩1 discounted at 10% over five years. The discount factor is applied to the value of the future benefit resulting in a present value of ₩142,830,000. This can be understood to mean that, "At a 10% discount rate, a benefit of ₩230,000,000 occurring five years from now has a present value of ₩140,530,000 (see Figure 7-2)."

In some analyses benefit or cost streams may be uniform over the duration of the project, with an annual cost or benefit of a certain amount. When this is the case, the discounting procedure can be simplified by summarizing the discounts for the various years in a single computation. Essentially an annuity factor, the present value of ₩1,000 received annually for n years can be computed with the formula

$$1-(1/1+r)^n/r$$

Where r again denotes the discount rate.

[Figure 7-2] Computing the Discount on a Single Benefit or Cost

Problem: Compute the present value of a ₩230,000,000 benefit expected to occur five years in the future, discounted by 10% per year.

Present value = discount factor × monetary benefit

Discount factor = $1/(1+r)^n$

$$= 1/(1+0.10)^5$$
$$= 1/1.6105$$
$$= 0.611$$

Present value $= 0.611 \times ₩230{,}000{,}000$
$= ₩140{,}530{,}000$

Figure 7-3 illustrates the calculation of the present value of a ₩90,000,000 annual cost over the next 20 years, using a 10% discount rate. First the annuity factor is computed using the formula above, then this is applied to the monetary valuc of the annual cost. The result is read as: "The present value of an annual cost of ₩90,000,000 over the next 20 years, discounted at 10% is ₩766,260,000."

[Figure 7-3] Computing the Discount on a Uniform Annual Benefit or Cost

Problem: Compute the present value of an annual cost of ₩90,000,000 over the next 20 years, discounted by 10% per year.

Present value = annuity discount factor × annual monetary value

Annuity factor $= 1- (1/1+r)^n/r$

$= 1-(1/1+0.10)^{20}/0.10$
$= 8.514$

Present value $= 8.514 \times ₩90{,}000{,}000$
$= ₩766{,}260{,}000$

Discussion Questions

1. What are the elements of CBA?
2. What are the steps of CBA?
3. Why is present value the standard for comparing monetary values?
4. What is the most appropriate discount rate?

Vocabulary

CBA
objective
alternative
cost
model
criterion
implement
feasibility
deteriorate
real
pecuniary
direct
indirect
internal
external
fixed
recurring
investment
monetary
monetary value
consumer surplus
compensation
discount rate
present value
private rate
social rate

References

Dunn, N. William (1994). *Public Policy Analysis: An Introduction.* Prentice-Hall: Englewood Cliffs, NJ.

Freeman, A. Myrick III (2000). "Economics, Incentives, and Environmental Regulation" in *Environmental Policy,* 4th ed. Edited by Norman J. Vig and Michael E. Kraft. CQ Press: Washington, DC.

"Korean-Language Proficiency Drops"
http://english.chosun.com/w21data/html/news/200807/200807030019.html

Kraft, E. Michael, and Furlong, R. Scott (2004). *Public Policy: Politics, Analysis, and Alternatives.* CQ Press: Washington, DC.

Weimer, L. David, and Vining, R. Aidan (2005). *Policy Analysis: Concepts and Practice.* Pearson Prentice Hall: Englewood Cliffs, NJ.

WEEK 8 Cost-Benefit Analysis(CBA) Ⅱ

Summary

There are many difficulties in measuring costs and benefits. The mathematical calculations always include various assumptions and judgments, including the choice of rates for calculating discount to present value.

Uncertainty is a major area for making judgments. It is addressed through contingency, sensitivity, and a fortiori analysis, as well as through assigning probabilities, and shadow pricing. Intangible costs and benefits are dealt with through means like comparable prices, consumer choice, derived demand, social surveys, and the cost of compensation. It is difficult, but sometimes necessary to place a monetary value on the cost of a human life. This is a controversial issue to deal with.

32 Comparing Costs and Benefits

There are as many variations of cost-benefit models as there are different ways of expressing the choice set and various procedures for selecting the preferred alternative. Here is a summary of one application of cost-benefit analysis to illustrate how the various classes of costs and benefits can be pulled together in order to compare alternatives.

Highway Project Illustration

This case pertains to hypothetical highway project in which two alternative expansion levels are considered in comparison with the no-build alternative, retaining the existing facility at the pre-expansion level. In this application the alternatives are compared incrementally, so that the benefits and costs of first expansion level, F_1, are derived by comparing it with the pre-expansion level, F_0, and those corresponding to the second expansion level, which might be a six-lane facility.

The illustration is instructive by its deficiencies as well as its stronger points. Only the most direct costs and benefits are taken into account: the benefits of time savings and other variable (operating) costs and costs of construction amd maintenance. If there is a bias in these computations, it is likely to be in favor of justifying one of the expansion levels, because of the exclusion of real secondary costs.

As shown in Table 8-1, the value of time savings is set at ₩2,000 per hour, and as the average time spent per trip declines dramatically with the first expansion level and then modestly as we move to the second expansion level, the average time cost per trip (line 2) decreases accordingly. Other trip costs increase slightly at the first expansion level, because of higher and less efficient operating speeds, and then decrease slightly at the second expansion level because of improved maneuverability in dispersed traffic. Total variable

[Table 8-1] Benefit-Cost Computations for Highway Project

		Pre-expansion Level F_0	After expansion to F_1	After expansion to F_2
Estimation of benefits to users				
1.	Time per trip (min)	30	18	16
2.	Time cost of trip (₩2,000/hr)	₩1,000	₩570	₩530
3.	Other cost per trip	₩1,750	₩1,900	₩1,850
4.	Total variable cost per trip			
	(2.+3.)	₩2,750	₩2,470	₩2,380
5.	Number of trips per year	1,000,000	1,500,000	1,750,000
5a.	Increase in trips		500,000	250,000
6.	Total variable costs per year			
	(4.×5.)	₩2,750,000,000	₩3,705,000,000	₩4,165,000,000
7.	Cost savings per trip		₩280	₩135
8.	Cost savings on previous no. of trips		₩280,000,000	₩135,000,000
9.	Cost savings on additional trips			
	$\left(\frac{1}{2}(7.\times 5a.)\right)$		₩70,000,000	₩16,875,000
10.	Total benefits per year			
	(8+9)		₩350,000,000	₩151,875,000
11.	Present value of benefits			
	(8%, 25 years)		₩3,736,172,000	₩1,621,232,000b
	Estimation of project cost			

12.	Capital lost		₩2,000,000,000	₩2,000,000,000
13.	Annual maintenance cost	₩20,000,000	₩30,000,000	₩50,000,000
14.	Increase in maintenance cost		₩10,000,000	₩20,000,000
15.	Present value of maintenance cost (8%, 25 years)		₩106,748,000	₩213,496,000
16.	Total project cost, present value (12+15)		₩2,106,748,000	₩2,213,496,000
	Evaluation			
17.	Benefit-cost ratio (line 11/line 16)		1.77	0.73

[a]Computation of direct benefits and cost only, moving incrementally from existing highway facility, F_0, to expansion level F_1, and then from F_1 to expansion level F_2.

[b]Computation as follows: $1-(1/1+0.08)^{25}/0.08$ (₩151,875,000) = ₩1,561,186,000

cost per trip (line 4) also follows the pattern of a dramatic decrease at the first expansion level and a much lesser decrease at the second expansion level.

Next, the total number of trips per year using the facility is taken into account, showing the additional volume of travel induced by the advantage of quicker travel. (Obviously the structural relationships between the facility's capacity and travel characteristics that underlie these computations are critical. This illustration shows only the summary of costs and benefits.) An additional 500,000 annual trips are forecast to be generated by the first expansion level and an additional 250,000 annual trips beyond that are forecast for the second expansion level.

The cost computations are less complex. The cost of constructing the facility to first expansion level specifications is estimated at ₩2 billion, and that for moving to the second expansion level is ₩2 billion more. Maintenance costs will increase from ₩20,000,000 to ₩30,000,000 per year for the first expansion level and up to ₩50,000,000 for the second expansion level. No effort is made to represent the greater maintenance needs that will be incurred later in the project's life as more than routine preventive maintenance measures are required. Total project costs are arrived at by discounting the cost of maintenance by 8% over the 25 years and adding this to the present value of construction costs.

Finally, the ratio of benefits to costs is calculated for each expansion level, with the results showing that moving beyond that to the second expansion level will incur costs that outweigh the additional benefits to be obtained. Regarding the second expansion level, the question is sometimes posed as to whether the investment would be more attractive if a toll were to be charged for use of the roadway, thereby reducing the net costs of the facility. The answer is "no" as this would constitute a pecuniary benefit, a transfer of money from the users to the authority operating the highway.

Furthermore, imposing a toll would actually be expected to lead to a reduction in net benefits because it would increase average trip costs, resulting in decreased usage of the facility.

33 Specialized Measurement Problems

Several ways of addressing the problems of measuring costs and benefits are described here. This is to help achieving workable results in the face of inherent uncertainties.

Treatment of Uncertainty

The problem of uncertainty is one of the major difficulties in an applied benefit-cost analysis. The way in which uncertainties are resolved can be the primary determinant of the results. Uncertainties are often dealt with in an arbitrary fashion, but in some cases more systematic treatments are possible. To understand the problem of dealing with uncertainties it is necessary to distinguish among various sources of uncertainty. Monetary values of impacts and appropriate discount rates are two classes of uncertainties.

The first problem comes largely from a lack of understanding of individual and group preferences. This is a normative issue. Other uncertainties relate to the impacts. Considering the highway example this might concern issues like:

- How much additional travel will be induced by the new facilities?
- By how much will accident rates and travel times be reduced?
- Will actual vehicle operating costs increase or decrease?
- What maintenance efforts will be required?
- What will be happened to fuel prices in the future and how will that affect the travel volumes?
- Will the speed limit change?
- Will noise levels actually be increased or reduced? Will there be any other positive or adverse environmental effects?
- Will there be any spin-offs on local economies?
- In the long run will land use patterns change so as to affect travel volumes on the facility?

Difficulties in estimating costs and benefits in substantive terms stem on three sources of uncertainty. The first involves uncertainty about cause/effect relationships between programs or projects and benefits and costs. It depends on the state of knowledge about observed effects of similar programs or projects in the past and is thus the primary focus of most ex post facto program or project evaluations. In the highway example projections of future benefits are based in part on past findings regarding the amount of additional travel that is generated by the opening of new highways. The more complete and situation-specific the past research findings, the better able we are to estimate future impacts of a given proposal.

The second source of uncertainty involves the question of whether observed or apparent relationships will hold for the future as well as uncertainty about future outcome steps of controlling environmental factors. Can additional travel be expected to develop on new highways in the future at the same rate at which this phenomenon has been observed in the past? Furthermore, will fuel prices or speed limits (environmental factors beyond the control of the transportation planners) be altered dramatically, exerting in turn an influence on travel volume? Addressing these issues requires attempts at fore-casting trends and making judgments about probable changes in the future.

The third type of uncertainty is statistical uncertainty rela-ting to the chance effect. This is the random component of experimental error, sometimes referred to as risk instead of uncertainty. This last category can be disposed of most easily as many quantitative techniques are available to deal with risk-inferential statistics as well as operations research probability models as discussed in other chapters. These should be employed where relevant. However, it should be noted that if the problem is swamped with uncertainty about cause/effect patterns and the nature of future outcome states, elaborate statistical treatments of chance effects may be of little use. Although uncertainties by definition will reduce the precision of a benefit-cost model, their implications fro the overall worthiness of a proposal can be taken into account with the following approaches.

Contingency Analysis

One strategy is to investigate how the ranking of the alternatives is affected by the assumption of contingency plans for the changes in environmental constraints. For example, a construction project might be costed at a specified amount, given an assumption of normal working conditions. In the event of unanticipated difficulties in excavation or a sudden increased in the const of materials, the estimated cost might be overrun considerably. That would this do to the benefit-cost ratio? Similarly, a local unit of government might be evaluating the benefits and costs of a new program for which national grants are available. It may base its costs on the local share only. If the national assistance is eliminated, what is the effect on the program's net benefits?

Sensitivity Analysis

Estimates of benefits and costs are often based on point projections of the level of some important environmental variable that is known to fluctuate considerably. Rather than working with expected values only, a more conservative approach is to develop projections based on both high and low levels to produce interval estimates of costs and benefits.

A Fortiori Analysis

A fortiori means for a stronger reason. This strategy is appropriate in situations in which intuitive judgment favors one alternative, X, while the objective analysis seems to point toward a second alternative, Y. With a fortiori analysis, the analyst arbitrarily resolves all uncertainties of any consequence in favor of X. If Y still emerges as the most advantageous alternative in benefit-cost terms, there is a much stronger case for this alternative. An example would be a choice between a new expressway and a rapid rail line in a transportation corridor. The two major uncertainties, fuel prices and parking availability could be set at levels continuing to seem advantageous. It would be a stronger indication that rapid rail cannot complete in that situation.

Assigning Probabilities

A fourth procedure is to assign probabilities to various outcome states, based on subjective judgment, probability sampling, or forecasting models. For instance, the benefits to be derived from a job training program will be partially dependent on the condition of the local labor market when the program is completed. If the analyst can derive some reasonable probabilities that the demand for the skills being developed will be high, moderate, or low, they can gain further insight as to the probable worth of the program.

It has also been pointed out that analysis of uncertainties using the above techniques may be of use in developing new alternatives. Through an examination of the impact of uncertainties, the analysis may gain a further understanding of the really critical, least controllable uncertainties. This could lead to the design of a new alternative that would "provide a reasonable good hedge against a range of the more significant uncertainties."

Shadow Pricing

Tangible benefits and costs in general are measured by their market prices, as these usually provide the best indication of what people are willing to pay for the use of resources. However, if observed prices are distorted by market imperfections, they will not represent true social values and costs and thus may have to be adjusted. Such adjustments are often termed shadow prices, corrections made to represent more accurately substitution ratios among resources or products or the real consequences of an investment decision in terms of alternative uses and opportunity costs.

There are many sources of market price distortion that might have to be adjusted of in a given benefit-cost analysis. In general, any restrictions on competition, such as monopoly or oligopoly conditions, restrictions on imports, or limited entry into an industry or occupation, may limit the supply of an input and inflate prices to levels above actual costs plus a normal rate of return. The real opportunity cost of the use of such inputs would be measured by the value of the product resulting from the alternative employment of the same factors of production in a competitive situation without excess profits.

Indirect taxes and price support programs also inflate market prices above the opportunity costs of the factors of production.

A nation with unemployed or underemployed resources can create measurement difficulties in a recession or depression. The usual assumption of benefit-cost analysis is that all resources used in a program of project, particularly labor, will be used elsewhere if the project is not undertaken. If this is not the case, there is no opportunity cost incurred by using them to undertaken the project.

The prospect of unemployment can also affect benefit computations. Employment opportunities afforded by a project are usually not counted as benefits because it is assumed that if the project is not undertaken, the funds will be invested and comparable employment opportunities will still be provided. If this is not the case, however, perhaps the income derived from employment in the project should be reckoned as a benefit. In assessing the consequence of halting a highway construction program in the US, for example, the loss of construction jobs would probably be taken into account because most of the funds are federal monies earmarked for highways. If the construction program is phased out, these funds would be forfeited by the state altogether, resulting in a real decrease in income in the state.

Use of Shadow Prices

The kinds of price distortions mentioned above can introduce serious biases in benefit-cost calculations and in certain applications should be adjusted for in order to reflect true opportunity costs. This cataloging should not suggest, however, that shadow prices are always preferable to observed market prices. With respect to observed prices that are distorted by market restrictions, for example, it has been argued that if such restrictions are anticipated to remain binding in the future, observed prices provide a more accurate indication of opportunity cost or sacrifice. Similarly, in terms of changing supply and demand conditions, if price changes attributable to independent factors or over the project itself can be forecast, they should be taken into account. The appropriate prices to use depend on the anticipated real world situation at the time the inputs are to be used.

Market distortions create discrepancies between purely economic valuations and financial appraisals, the former representing opportunity costs in terms of technological relationships and the latter representing money outlays based on market prices. Money outlays certainly represent opportunity costs too, in the sense of how much of other kinds of inputs cannot be purchased if a given project is undertaken. In general, projects should be undertaken only if justified.

Intangible Costs and Benefits

Intangibles are much more difficult to measure in monetary values because there is no direct market experience to serve as the basis for the valuation. Benefit-cost analysis seeks to measure all impacts in monetary terms as they would be valued by the affected parties. The problem is that the preferences of the affected parties for intangibles are not revealed in the market. Some intangibles are readily quantifiable, such as psychological stress engendered by driving in heavy traffic. Rather than affixing monetary values to them, the former type may be summarized quantitatively in substantive measures and the latter type summarized descriptively as a complement to the benefit-cost computations. This is certainly preferable to ignoring them altogether, which can severely bias the conclusions to be drawn, but the use of different measuring units necessarily precludes the possibility of arriving at single measure of net benefit.

The alternative is to attempt to impute monetary values to intangible costs and benefits through indirect approaches. This has the advantage of expressing the value of all costs and benefits in a common unit of measurement, but often the methods for imputing monetary values to intangibles are based on tenuous assumptions, hinging the analysis on questionable measures. This can be crucial, especially when the more prominent impacts are intangibles. For example, one of the major benefits attributed to most transportation improvements is savings in travel time, but there is a notable lack of consensus on how such time should be valued. The effect of using an average value of ₩2,750 per hour as opposed to ₩2,500 per hour can easily be the difference between justifying and rejecting a project.

Comparable Prices

One way of imputing monetary values to intangibles is to observe price relationships for similar items in the market. A frequent application of this approach is the use of area wage rates as the value of time saved in travel because of the construction of a new transportation facility, equating travel time with work time. This is questionable even for working time (travel on the job) because travel time saved does not always represent a real gain in opportunity. Often the time saved is not converted into economic value. For nonworking time it is an even more doubtful measure. What are the opportunity costs of spending time in travel? Clearly there is wide range of answers to this question depending on what people could or would do instead of traveling and how much satisfaction they derive from these other activities. If the time saved from travel could be used to earn additional income, it has a certain value, but if the time is spent in leisure activity, its value may be quite different.

Consumer Choice Situations

A second approach to measuring the monetary value of intangibles is to observe consumer behavior in certain choice situations or experiments that provide clues as to how people value trade-offs between a given intangible and money. For example, an estimate of how commuters value their time can be derived by observing the choices they make between a less expensive, time consuming travel mode and a more expensive but quicker means of making the same trip.

However, such a measure is valid only if the consumers have complete information about the alternatives and if all other possible influences on the decision can be assumed to be natural or accounted for in some way. In the example the commuters would have know the time consequences of the alternatives, and the two travel modes would have to be alike in all other respects. If there is difference in comfort between the two, the choices observed cannot necessarily be attributed solely to time and cost considerations.

Furthermore, there may be difficulty in inferring that the same trade-offs apply to a larger group of consumers. For example, if the experiment involved the choice between express and local subway trains, there would be no assurance that the monetary value established would pertain to commuters in general, other than subway users.

Derived Demand

In some situations the demand curve for a service or facility provided for free can be derived by computing indirect costs. For example, consider a large state park for which there is no entry free. Users come from different locations and thus incur different costs in reaching the park. Fewer visitors come from farther away because of the higher costs to them. If it can be assumed that the trip has no other purpose and no inherent utility, the travel demand is derived from the desire to visit the park, and the travel costs incurred can be considered to represent the actual prices paid to use the park.

This information can be used to develop a measure of the satisfaction received by visitors to the park, a final benefit for which no direct monetary valuation is available. Zones around the park can be delineated according to average travel costs and the number of annual visitors per 1,000 residents can be computed for each zone. Aggregating the zones with different average travel costs will produce a demand curve for the park, and the usage rate will decline as the price rises. If the zones can be considered similar in terms of the preference of their residents for use of the park, the demand curve can be applied to each zone separately and compared with actual usage. The difference between this demand curve and the flat price (the average travel cost from the zone to the park) for those people who so do visit the park will represent the consumer surplus, the difference between the costs actually incurred in getting to the park and what the visitors would be willing to pay to use the park if they had to.

Social Surveys

A different approach to imputing monetary values to intangibles is to ask people how they value a certain service. This can be used to replicate an experiment in consumer choice, but it involves additional threats to validity. For instance, to evaluate the benefits of a proposed new bus route, a survey might be used go ask potential riders how many trips per week they would make on the route at varying fare levels. The demand curve so generated can be compared with the proposed flat fare, with the recognition, however, that people tend to inflate their response in such surveys. In general the validity of the monetary value estimates is subject to all the measurement problems associated with survey research.

Cost of Compensation

Sometimes costs, particularly negative externalities, can be valued by pricing out what it would actually cost to physically overcome them. For example, the costs of detrimental physical environmental impacts of a project might be valued in monetary terms by the direct costs of mounting the necessary abatement programs to return to the noise levels and air quality that prevailed before construction of the project.

Using similar logic in reverse, the monetary value of benefits produced by a public health program that provides free inoculations against and anticipated epidemic might be imputed from cost avoided. Theoretically, the benefits are worth whatever people would be willing to pay for them, but in practice they might be evaluated by estimates of potential medical costs and lost earnings that were avoided by virtue of being protected against the disease in question.

Value of Human Life

The difficulties involved in trying to place a monetary value of the saving of a human life, or the loss human life, illustrate well the frustration of coming to grips with intangibles in economic analysis. A number of alternative approaches have been developed - based on projected earnings, the monetary value implied by governmental policies, insurance premiums paid, etc. - but they all raise as many questions as they answer. Yet, many programs, such as police protection, highway safety, health care, and ambulance services, are aimed in part at saving human lives, and their evaluation in large part hinges on this question.

It should be pointed out that although there is much interest in devising methodologies for placing monetary values on intangible costs and benefits, one school of thought cautions that this may not be desirable. This position holds that if there is no clear indication of the values people place in impacts based on market experience, they can be evaluated only through budget determination by the political process. The principles of economic analysis can then be applied to a more limited problem constrained by the specification to be tolerated or avoided. This approach, referred to as cost-effectiveness is discussed in the following section.

Discussion Questions

1. What are the difficulties in resolving questions of uncertainty?
2. How can different preferences in using money be fairly compared?
3. How can we place a monetary value on human life?

Vocabulary

uncertainty
contingency analysis
sensitivity
a fortiori
probability
shadow pricing
financial appraisal
intangible cost and benefit
comparable price
consumer choice
derived demand
social surveys
cost of compensation
value of human life

References

Dunn, N. William (1994). *Public Policy Analysis: An Introduction.* Prentice-Hall: Englewood Cliffs, NJ.

Freeman, A. Myrick III (2000). "Economics, Incentives, and Environmental Regulation" in *Environmental Policy,* 4th ed. Edited by Norman J. Vig and Michael E. Kraft. CQ Press: Washington, DC.

"Korean-Language Proficiency Drops"
http://english.chosun.com/w21data/html/news/200807/200807030019.html

Kraft, E. Michael, and Furlong, R. Scott (2004). *Public Policy: Politics, Analysis, and Alternatives.* CQ Press: Washington, DC.

Weimer, L. David, and Vining, R. Aidan (2005). *Policy Analysis: Concepts and Practice.* Pearson Prentice Hall: Englewood Cliffs, NJ.

WEEK 9 Cost-Effectiveness Analysis(CEA)

Summary

Cost-effectiveness analysis(CEA) is an alternative to cost-benefit analysis. It is used especially where the decision is not whether or not to take action, but where action must be taken, as in health and safety. The task is to select an alternative where the choice is the most effective among a range of choices.

Fixed utility is a way of comparing costs at the same level of effectiveness.

Fixed budget is the most common method. It compares benefits at the same level of expenditure.

The Concept of Cost-Effectiveness Analysis(CEA)

Sometimes concerns about the ability to measure the benefits of a policy action are so significant that cost-benefit analysis is not helpful. In such cases as where health regulations, highway safety, or medical research may prevent disease, devastating injury, or save lives there is the question of how analysts place a monetary value on human lives and health. Government agency officials and analysts, along with insurance companies, have methods for estimating how much a life is worth, even though many critics object in principle to making such calculations.

The advantage of cost-effectiveness analysis is that it requires no measurements of the value of intangible benefits such as human lives. Instead, it simply compares different policy alternatives that can produce these benefits in terms of their relative costs. That is, analysts ask which actions can save the most human lives given a fixed monetary cost, or which monetary investments produce the greatest benefits.

This kind of comparison is also common in safety and environmental regulation, where the cost of the regulations in terms of lives that would be saved is often ten, one hundred, or even one thousand times greater than other actions that could be taken. In these circumstances, critics of regulation cite the wide disparities in costs to argue against the adoption of targeted measures. For example, improving workplace safety or eliminating toxic chemicals from the environment may be very expensive in terms of relative effectiveness in achieving the policy's goals. Therefore, they suggest that the same benefits might be achieved by taking other, sometimes far cheaper, policy actions.

[Box 9-1] Effective English

Writing for *Chosun Ilbo* on February 14, 2008, Moon Gabsik calculated the cost of English language test preparation in Gangnam at ₩263.5 billion a year, not including transportation, textbook, and snacks.

The ratio of private education by subject is 100 for English, 50 for math, and 25 for Korean based on the weight English occupies in the private education market.

Moon says a short cut to reducing English private education costs is to eliminate English from thc college entrance exams. It would transform painful language study into enjoyable lessons.

The private English education market already has a large number of native-speaking teachers because parents and students prefer them.

At the same time, South Koreans (who spend lots of money on studying for English tests) earn only slightly higher scores than North Koreans do.

Foreigners also frequently complain that, for all of the Koreans crazed with getting a high TOEIC score, they have difficulty actually communicating with Koreans in English.

What is the proper balance in learning English?

Discussion Questions

- How well is the money spent on learning English in Korea? Could it be spent more effectively?
- Should Korean education spend more time on practical English than on preparing for tests?
- How much English do Koreans really need to know?

– Chosun Ilbo

35 CEA Approaches

The use of cost-effectiveness analysis is necessary to address questions that are not feasible for benefit-cost analysis applications in an operational sense or are too constrained for the scope of benefit-cost analysis. This is the case with social goods. Where the product is of a collective nature shared in equal amounts by all citizens, such as national defense or clean air and water, a good is called a social good.

People do not reveal their preferences for more or less national defense in the economic marketplace, and the benefits of defense programs are not measured in monetary terms. In analyzing the deployment of strategic forces, for example, effectiveness might be measured in terms of the numbers of particular types of forces which can be deployed to specific areas by a specific time. Alternative sites of basing such forces could then be compared both in terms of this measure of effectiveness and the costs of transporting the forces.

Second, cost-effectiveness has been found to be an attractive approach to problems characterized by major externalities or intangibles. An externality is a factor that is not included inside the policy or program, but is a cost or benefit that is outside of the program calculation. When a corporation calculates the costs and benefits of building a new factory, pollution is an externality unless it is part of an environmental impact statement that has been monetarized and added into the costs. An intangible is a cost or benefit that can not be seen, felt, or readily measured. The increase in community pride associated with a new stadium is an intangible effect.

Where these factors cannot readily be measured in monetary terms as required by benefit-cost analysis, they can be dealt with substantively in cost-effectiveness analysis, either by setting them equivalent across the alternatives or by holding the alternatives to constraints set in terms of intangibles. In developing an industrial park or airport, for example, rather than attempting to put monetary values on negative impacts above certain specified levels. Those alternatives are then compared in the traditional benefit-cost format. Selection of the preferred alternative plan will be based on differences in the tangible factors only. As a result there may be no precise indication of their true net worth.

[Figure 9-1] National Defense is a Public Good

This K-1 tank is an example of a defense option that is often considered under a fixed budget approach. Different options that have equal effectiveness are compared on the basis of price and the least costly option is selected.

Fixed Utility

Sometimes there is no ability to determine real net benefit. In such cases alternative program strategies are often compared by holding the level of effectiveness constant. Then the analysts compare differences in their costs. This is the fixed utility approach. They may also hold costs constant and compare levels of effectiveness. This is the fixed budget approach.

The fixed utility approach is commonly used in national defense analysis. A specific level of military deterrent capability may be established and alternative systems analyzed in terms of both deterrent capability and costs. The cost-effective alternative is the one that meets the level of effectiveness at least cost. For example, the army decides that one K-1 tank has the same combat power as 150 soldiers. The army then procures the cheapest option.

There are lots of examples of the usefulness of the fixed utility approach. A city planning department may set the objective of reducing the number of families housed in substandard dwelling units by 50%. They compare the costs of attaining this objective through the construction of new housing and the rehabilitation of existing housing. Differences in social or psychological effects should also be noted and adjusted for, if possible, to ensure the validity of the comparison.

It should be understood that fixed utility will not always refer to final impacts in the sense in which the term effectiveness is used in this text, but rather the fixed utility may also be set in terms of intermediate effects and outputs. In essence then, the cost-effective alternative would be that which produces the specified type and level of outputs at least cost.

Fixed Budget

Cost-effectiveness analysis is perhaps used more frequently in the allocation of fixed budget amounts. After all, governments and businesses usually have specific budget limits. Resource allocation decisions made within budget constraints answer the question addressed by benefit-cost analysis. That is, how many resources should be invested in a program or project? In such a context benefit-cost principles can be used to find the best solution within the budget constraint.

Assume a fixed budget to be allocated between two program categories. The two categories should be funded where their marginal benefits are equal. This will maximize the effectiveness of the program as a whole. This does not examine the more important question of whether the budget should be augmented or cut, with funds diverted to other programs. The use of the internal rate of return method has also been advocated for this kind of context. For example, it is used in allocating job training program funds between programs teaching general skills and those teaching specialized skills. The internal rate of return is a calculation of the percentage return on investment of a program. If one program's rate of return is higher than that of another, funds should be shifted from the first to the second until the point where the economic marginal returns are equalized.

With respect to operating programs, the fixed budget approach may be used more often than the fixed utility approach. The actual program constraints are frequently budget constraints. It is also widely used because the available data often make this method easier to carry out. For example, if a metropolitan city government had experimented with a car utilization plan and found that it was associated with a 10% decrease in the certain types of personnel complaints, it can measure the cost-effectiveness of that strategy by relating this observed effect to the cost of implementing the plan. It is easier for the city to compare this performance with the performance of other strategies such as a new work schedule or an enhanced employee benefits program, for example, by using a fixed budget than by calculating the level of effectiveness of each strategy independently. Holding costs constant is easier than trying to obtain exactly the same degree of effectiveness with each strategy. The city can invest the same amount of funds spent on the fleet plan in each of the other two strategies, separately, and then compare the percent decrease in complaints associated with each of the three alternatives.

Air Pollution Example

Grit is a kind of air pollution released by factory smokestacks. Installing grit-arresting equipment produces the good freedom from air pollution. This good can be measured in units of grit and dust arrested.

Table 9-1 shows the marginal cost per metric ton, of arresting grit and dust at each power station for each of a range of levels of efficient of the equipment installed. With the 98.8% efficient equipment actually installed at the two stations, the marginal cost is 113 pounds per metric ton at A and 225 pounds per metric ton at B.

A rational government would seek to achieve that level of pollution control at which the marginal cost of preventing a unit of pollution from occurring is just equal to the marginal social value of freedom from pollution (MC = MR). Thus the decision that station A should have 98.8% efficient equipment implies a judgment that the marginal social value of freedom from pollution is 113 pounds per metric ton of grit and dust arrested. The decision that station B should have 98.8% efficient equipment implies a judgment that the marginal social value of freedom from pollution is 225 pounds per metric ton arrested. The two decisions are not consistent.

[Table 9-1] Grit Arrested in Two Factories, A and B

Efficiency	Cost	Mass Arrested A	Mass Arrested B	Marginal Cost of Efficiency	Marginal Cost per Ton Arrested A	Marginal Cost per Ton Arrested B
98.0%	40.9	7840	3920	-	-	-
98.2%	42.0	7856	3928	5.5	69	138
98.4%	43.2	7872	3936	6.0	75	150
98.6%	44.7	7888	3944	7.5	94	188
98.8%	46.5	7904	3952	9.0	113	225
98.9%	47.5	7912	3956	10.0	125	250
99.0%	48.6	7920	3960	11.0	138	275
99.1%	49.8	7928	3964	12.0	150	300
99.2%	51.4	7936	3968	16.0	200	400

The marginal social value of preventing the emission of grit and dust that is implied by each of the two decisions:

Station A = 113 pounds

Station B = 225 pounds

At this point the marginal cost is the same as the marginal value.

The combined effect of these two decisions is that 11,856 metric tons of grit (7904 + 3952) and dust are arrested each year at a combined cost of 93,000 pounds (46,500 + 46,500) per year. By making different decisions it would be possible to arrest more grit and dust at the same cost (or to arrest the same quantity at lower cost).

For example, by installing a 99.1% efficient equipment at A and 98.4% equipment at B, 11,864 (7928 + 3936) metric tons per year are arrested at the same total cost of 93,000 pounds per year (49,800 + 43,200). Both of these decisions imply the same marginal social value of freedom from pollution: 150 pounds per metric ton of grit and dust arrested.

A pair of decisions about the levels of efficiency of the equipment to be installed at the two power stations:

Station A: 99.1% (MC = MR = 150)

Station B: 98.4% (MC = MR = 150)

Discussion Questions

1. How is CEA better than CBA?
2. Why is CEA more useful in many environmental, health, and safety regulations?
3. Why is it generally better for the public sector to provide social goods?
4. When is fixed utility more useful than a fixed budget approach? Give a real-world example.

Vocabulary

comparison
CEA
externality
intangible
prioritize
social goods
fixed utility
fixed budget
internal rate of return

References

"Don't Railroad Changes to English Teaching Through" http://english.chosun.com/w21data/html/news/200802/200802140012.html

Dunn, N. William (1994). *Public Policy Analysis: An Introduction.* Prentice-Hall: Englewood Cliffs, NJ.

Freeman, A. Myrick III (2000). "Economics, Incentives, and Environmental Regulation," in *Environmental Policy,* 4th ed. Edited by Norman J. Vig and Michael E. Kraft. CQ Press: Washington, DC.

Kraft, E. Michael, and Furlong, R. Scott (2004). *Public Policy: Politics, Analysis, and Alternatives.* CQ Press: Washington, DC.

"N. Koreans Fare No Worse on TOEFL Than S. Koreans" http://english.chosun.com/w21data/html/news/200802/200802150018.html

Weimer, L. David, and Vining, R. Aidan (2005). *Policy Analysis: Concepts and Practice.* Pearson Prentice Hall: Englewood Cliffs, NJ.

WEEK 10 Risk Assessment, Decision Analysis, and Others

Summary

Risk assessment is used to consider risks to citizens. It is considered through the formula R = PC. R is the risk, P is the probability of an event, and C represents the bad consequences of the event.

Decision analysis is a way of organizing decisions that involve uncertainty. A decision tree is a way of constructing a flow chart for visually organizing a complex sequence of decisions.

Forecasting is the process of rationally determining the likely future consequences of a policy. Forecasting is the element that allows policy analysts to exercise some control over the future.

Forecasts may be projections of current and past trends, predictions based on the best information available, or conjectures based on experienced judgment.

An impact assessment is a kind of forecast that tries to consider the effects and consequences of a course of action. This is particularly useful in planning to mitigate negative consequences.

Political feasibility analysis determines the probability of

political action on a policy proposal. While there is no exact formula, the process involves identifying the key policy actors, their position, level of involvement, motivation, and level of concern regarding the issue at hand. Small groups can have a disproportionate impact on the process.
Ethical analysis compares policy proposals against ethical standards like regime values, or common legal and philosophical ethics in society.

36 Risk Assessment

Risk assessment is a close relative of cost-benefit analysis.

[Figure 10-1] Airbags are a Way of Decreasing Risk

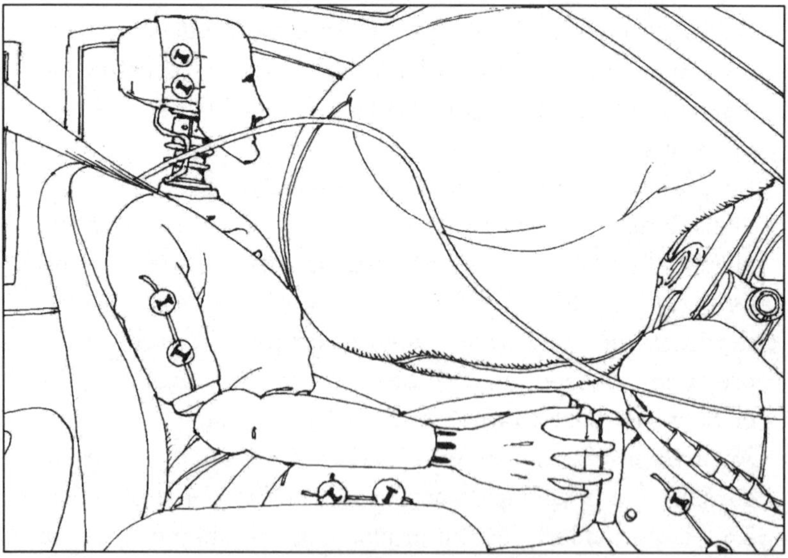

There are two approaches to reducing risk, decreasing probability and reducing consequences. Airbags decrease risk through reducing the consequences of an accident.

The purpose of risk assessment is to identify, estimate, and evaluate the magnitude of the risk to citizens from exposure to various situations. Reduced risk conveys a benefit to the public. Risk is usually defined as the probability and severity of adverse consequences of an event or exposure. The event may be an typhoon, a car accident, a nuclear power plant mishap, or an earthquake, and exposure to risk could come through contaminated food, water, or air, or being in or near a building or other structure that is damaged.

The equation $R = P \times C$ expresses that risk is a product of the probability that the event or exposure will occur and the consequences that follow if it does. Here,

R = Risk
P = The probability of the event or exposure.
C = The consequences of the event or exposure.

Some risks, such as an airplane crash, have a low probability of occurring but high consequences if they do. Others, such as a broken leg from a snowboarding accident, have a higher probability, but have lower consequences.

Variety of Risks

Risks vary widely. They may be associated with driving a car, flying in an airplane, consuming a certain diet, smoking cigarettes, drinking alcohol, snowboarding, or suffering from a natural or manmade disaster, among others. Everyday life is filled with risks, but most are minor. Few are alarming, although people especially worry about technological risks, such as nuclear waste, hazardous waste, toxic chemicals, and radiation.

[Box 10-1] *Traffic Risk*

How great are the risks on Korea's roads? What are the consequences of those risks? On June 4, 2008, *Chosun Ilbo* reported that Korea's traffic accident fatality rate is more than twice as high as the average of OECD countries, ranking 27th out of 29 countries. The Ministry of Land, Transport, and Maritime Affairs reported that an average of 3.34 people died in traffic accidents for every 10,000 cars in Korea in 2006. This was more than double the OECD average of 1.53. Korea's figure dropped slightly to 3.08 in 2007 but still remains relatively high.

Switzerland had the lowest traffic accident fatality rate with 0.72 deaths per 10,000 cars, Japan had 0.88, Germany recorded 0.93, and the US was 20th with 1.74. Only Turkey and Hungary had fatality rates worse than Korea's.

The newspaper reported that in 2007, 6,166 people died in 211,662 traffic accidents, for an average of 16.9 deaths every day. Accidents happen most frequently in the evening between 6 pm and 10 pm. Weekends are also especially dangerous, with 14.8% of fatal accidents happening on Fridays and 16% on Saturdays.

Discussion Questions

- Why does Korea have so many accidents?
- Consider the formula $R = P \times C$ to determine how serious this issue is.
- What can be done to reduce traffic fatalities? Consider both probabilities and consequences.

– Chosun Ilbo

Risk assessments are used widely today in part because of public fears of technological risks and the adoption of public policies to control or reduce risks. Workplace safety and food safety are two examples. Risk assessments are also prepared to estimate and respond to national security risks, such as invasion, terrorist attacks or other threats to the country.

If risk assessment is the use of different methods to identify risks and estimate their probability and severity of harm, risk evaluation is a determination of the acceptability of the risks or a decision about what level of safety is desired. Both a higher level of safety and a lower level of risk cost more to achieve. Risk management describes what governments or other organizations do to deal with risks, such as adopting public policies to regulate them.

Analysts use many different methods to conduct risk assessments. These assessments range from estimating the likelihood of industrial accidents to calculating how much radioactivity is likely to leak from a nuclear waste repository over ten thousand years. For some assessments, such as the risk of auto accidents or the likely injury to children from deployment of air bags during an accident, the task is relatively easy because plenty of data exist on the actual experience of drivers, vehicles, and air bag deployment. As a result, insurance companies can figure out how much to charge for insurance once they know the age of the driver, what kind of car it is, and where and how far it is driven each day.

For other estimates, the lack of experience means that analysts must depend on mathematical modeling and computer projections. For example, computer modeling is used to project the risk of climate change and the consequences for a society if average temperatures rise, rainfall patterns shift, or severe

[Figure 10-2] Nuclear Waste May Pose a Potential Risk for Thousands of Years

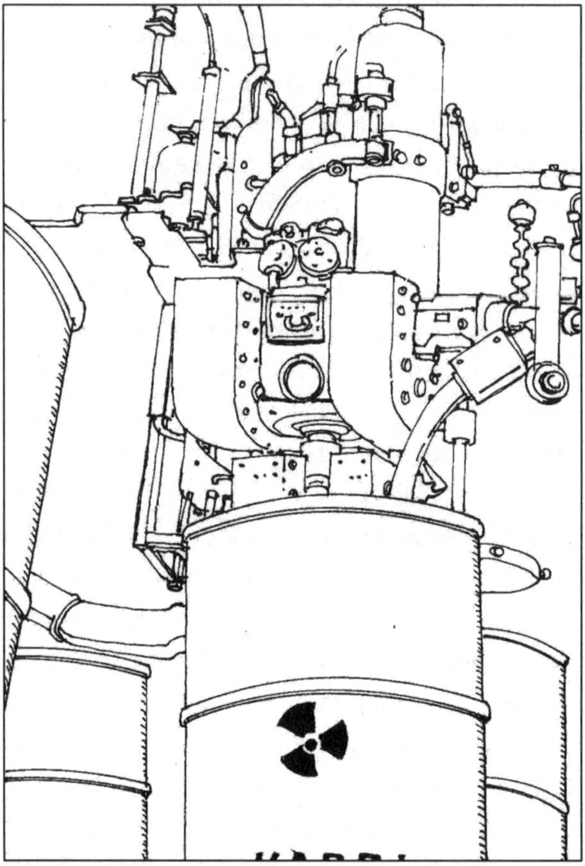

Technological risks are often perceived as greater because they are less well-understood by the public. They also pose special challenges in the calculation of risk.

storms occur more frequently. Risk assessment can identify genuine and serious risks that require public policy action. As with cost-benefit analysis, conservatives and business interests strongly favor the use of risk assessment methods for domestic policy conflicts.

37 Decision Analysis

What is decision analysis? Decision analysis provides us a way for dealing with uncertain and confusing situations. It provides a technique for finding the best route. Since the 1960s, businessmen have increasingly used decision analysis for tackling problems where decisions must be made sequentially and where uncertainty is a critical element.

Decision analysis combines some of the features of the other methods we have studied. This particularly includes an assessment of costs and benefits, but it uses a graphic portrayal of the available options to allow analysts to follow the consequences of each option. Basically, it is another way to consolidate and display information. This approach is useful as it provides a method to structure an analyst's thinking about the problems they are facing and the available alternatives.

Decision analysis is a formal way to structure possible decisions under conditions of uncertainty. Two or more alternatives can be sketched out in what is called a decision tree. Each branch of the tree portrays the consequences of choosing one of the alternatives, and each decision is associated with some degree of uncertainty and risk. Policy makers need to ask themselves whether they should choose the option with the least risk, even if the outcomes might be less attractive, or an option that carries greater risk or failure, but more favorable outcomes.

Most of the public policy issues for which decision analysis is useful are complex. They are far too complex for introducing the process.

An example that is easier to understand is presented below. The members of a university club decide to raise money by holding a dinner party. It is the rainy season and rains nine days out of ten. The students must decide whether to hold the dinner indoors or outdoors. A tent is available, but uncomfortable. Past experience has shown turnout to be low at indoor functions, resulting in a 60% chance of gaining ₩200,000 from a dinner held in the tent and a 40% per cent chance of losing ₩40,000. On the other hand, an outdoor dinner could be expected to earn ₩500,000 unless it rains, in which case the dinner would lose about ₩10,000.

The first step in using decision analysis to solve the club's problem is to diagram the sequence of decisions and chance events that it faces. The particular type of diagram that is used is called a decision tree. In Figure 10-3 there is a decision tree for this situation.

[Figure 10-3] Decision Tree

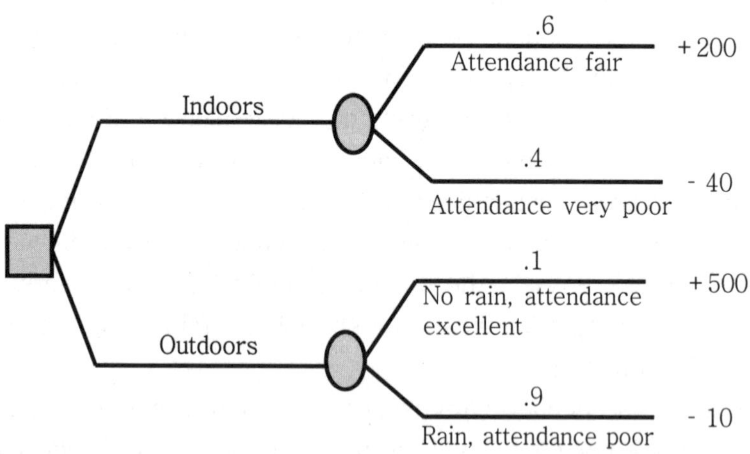

The first decision the club faces is whether to hold the party indoors or outdoors. At the left a square, or decision node, indicates that at this point a decision must be made. Two lines branch out of the decision node to show the two possible choices, and label them indoors and outdoors.

The club then asks what happens if they follow the upper branch, and hold the dinner indoors. The answer is that it all depends on chance. It depends on how many people come to the dinner. At the end of the "Indoors" branch is a circle or chance node, which indicates that at this point an uncertainty must be resolved.

At this chance node there are two possibilities: The party may be moderately successful (attendance fair), or it may be unsuccessful (attendance very poor). Therefore there are two branches for these possible results, and they are labeled accordingly. Moreover, for this decision problem we know the probabilities of these possible outcomes, for we are told that there is a 60% chance of the first and a 40% chance of the second. These numbers are recorded along the appropriate branches. Finally, we are also told that the gain from a moderately successful dinner is ₩200,000 while very poor attendance will result in the loss of ₩40,000. These are the ultimate outcomes or payoffs for each possible combination of choice and chance. They are shown at the end of the different branches.

Similarly, the two possibilities and probabilities for an outdoor dinner come from the lower chance node, along with the respective payoffs. The tree thus summarizes all the essential information that is available. Uncertainty is unavoidable in this situation. The decision must be made before the decision maker knows what the weather will be. The decision node comes before the chance nodes. This situation always requires close attention when a decision tree is drawn.

The problem as set forth has obviously been simplified. The club may have other options. They might do nothing. There may also be other weather possibilities, such as overcast. The club could try to get a reliable long-range weather forecast. They may also even pay some extra for the option of making the final decision a few hours before the dinner. Understanding the process is more important than a comprehensive view of the situation.

A decision tree is, then, a kind of flow chart that shows the logical structure of a decision problem. A decision tree helps communicate assumptions and valuations. It is a tool that facilitates sensible policy discussion. It contains four elements:

- Decision nodes
- Chance nodes
- Probabilities
- Payoffs

Decision nodes indicate all possible courses of action open to the decision maker.

Chance nodes show the intervening uncertainties and all their possible outcomes.

Probabilities show the chance of each possible outcome of a chance event.

Payoffs summarize the consequences of each possible combination of choice and chance.

However, decision analysis forces one to think carefully about:

- The true nature of the decision problem

- The role of chance
- The nature of the sequential interaction of decisions and chance events.

38 Forecasting

After a policy problem has been structured an analyst may forecast the future consequences of policy alternatives. Policy alternatives are partially contained in the original formulation of a problem. If poverty is defined as an economic problem, then economic alternatives (employment, income supplements, job training) will be considered as the alternatives. On the other hand, non-economic alternatives (affirmative action and equal employment opportunity) will be regarded as irrelevant in an economic formulation of the problem.

Public policy making would not be a very productive practice without accurate forecasts. Policy analysts can only hope to influence the future if they first come to understand it. Forecasting is not just necessary for social guidance. It also helps policy makers foresee and avoid unanticipated negative consequences of public policy. These kinds of consequences include pollution, energy shortages, and urban sprawl. Forecasting helps provide information that allows us to shape the future actively as well as react to changes projected from historical data. As a result, the future is a combination of trends from the past and the influences we place on those trends to guide them in a different direction.

Forecasting is using information from the past to predict the most likely courses of the future. Forecasting methods allow analysts to anticipate what the future is likely to hold based on their understanding of current conditions and how they expect them to change over time.

[Figure 10-4] A Weather Forecast is an Example of a Forecast

Forecasting is a method of producing factual information about future states of society on the basis of information about the nature of policy problems. Forecasts may take three principle forms: projections, predictions, and conjectures (see Table 10-1).

- A projection is a forecast made from an extrapolation of current and historical trends into the future. Projections make claims about the future. These claims are typically based on arguments from methods and parallel cases, where assumptions about the validity of particular methods (such as time-series analysis) or similarities between cases (as in past and future policies) are used to establish the claims. While projections may be supplemented by arguments from authority (using the opinions of experts), projections do not make use of other modes of policy argument.

- A prediction is a forecast based on explicit theoretical assumptions. These assumptions may take the form of theoretical laws (for example, the proposition that civil disorders are caused by the gap between expectations and capabilities), or analogies (for example, the analogy between the growth of government and the growth of biological organisms). The essential feature of a prediction is that it specifies the causes and effects. It may also establish parallel processes or relations, known as analogues, believed to underlie a relationship. While predictions may be supplemented by arguments from authority or method, they do not make use of other modes of policy argument.

- A conjecture is a forecast based on subjective judgments about the future. These judgments may take the form of intuitive arguments, where assumptions about the insight, creative intellectual power, or tacit knowledge of stakeholders (such as that of key decision makers) are used to support claims about the future. Judgments may also be expressed as arguments where present or future goals, values, and intentions of stakeholders are used to establish the claims, as when conjectures about future social values (for example, leisure) are used to claim that the average work week will be reduced to 36 hours in the next twenty years. While conjectures may be supplemented by arguments from authority or other methods, their essential feature is that they are based on subjective judgments, rather than on empirical data or scientific theories.

[Table 10-1] Three Forms of Policy Forecast

Form of Forecast	Basis of Forecast	Primary Focus of Supporting Argument
Projection	Current and Historical Trends	Method Parallel Case
Prediction	Theoretical Assumptions	Cause Analogy
Conjecture	Subjective Judgment	Insight Motivation

The population of South Korea was estimated at 48 million in 2004, but what will it be in twenty-five or fifty years? Projections of the nation's future population depend on a series of assumptions about the average number of children each woman is likely to have, the rate of immigration, and other factors.

Projections of population growth are a good example of what is usually called geometric or exponential growth. Such projections are easy to calculate once you know the rate of growth. It is the same equation used to determine compound interest:

$$A_n = P(1+i)^n$$

Where:

A = the projection
n = the number of years

P = the initial amount
i = the rate of growth

The formula is quite handy for determining how much a given amount will be in any number of years. A savings account in the amount of ₩100,000 (P) that earns four percent a year (i=4) will be worth ₩104,000 after one year (n=1), ₩126,532 at the end of five years (n=5), and W160,103 after ten years (n=10).

Considering a different example, in order to determine how much an apartment that is now valued at ₩200,000,000 will cost in ten years, you must determine what the annual rate of increase is likely to be (3%/5%/8%?) and the formula will provide the answer. At a 5% annual rate of increase, the apartment will cost ₩326,000,000 in ten years. As these examples illustrate, even a small rate of annual increase can produce great changes over time.

39 Impact Assessment

Impact assessment is a strategy of policy making and administration through analysis of predictable impacts. While it sounds very easy, it can be very sophisticated and can have a great subtlety in making powerful judgments.

Much like forecasting, the purpose of impact assessment is to systematically examine the possible effects of a particular action. No matter what the subject, the analyst tries to identify possible impacts and the likelihood they will occur.

[Box 10-2] **Korean Economic Projection: Stagflation**

Governments frequently use forecasting as a tool to predict future economic performance. The Bank of Korea announced July 1, 2008 that Korea's economic growth was projected to slow to 4.6% in 2008 from 5% in 2007 as surging oil prices reduced domestic demand, as reported by the *Korea Herald* on July 2.

The central bank also said the consumer price index was expected to hit a ten-year high in 2008. The inflation forecast increased over an earlier December prediction of 3.3% to 4.8%, the highest since the consumer price index hit 7.5% in 1998 during the Asian financial crisis.

The rapid surge in international oil prices and other raw materials and the global economic slowdown were factors considered in the projection.

Economic growth was also predicted to take a hit, dropping from 5.4% in the first half of the year to only 3.9% in the second half.

With lower growth and higher inflation, the policy debate was expected to shift from how to promote growth and create jobs to whether to emphasize a fight against inflation or economic growth. These are often seen as mutually exclusive policy goals.

Discussion Questions

- What kind of forecast methods did the Bank of Korea employ?
- How realistic is this assessment of Korea's economic future? Are there any other factors or conditions that should be considered?
- Is it more important to fight inflation, or is it more important to grow the economy?

– Korea Herald

[Figure 10-5] A Canal

The decision to build a canal may depend on the impact assessment. The canal project of President Lee was opposed on the basis of potential negative environmental impacts.

40 Political Feasibility Analysis

Political feasibility, a way of evaluating suggested policy changes, is the extent to which the various different policy actors will support the change. No formula is available for estimating political feasibility. Even experienced and thoughtful observers of politics acknowledge how difficult it is to determine the level of support for a proposal in local or central government. It may be easier to recognize the actions that are unlikely to be politically viable. Some simple determinations can provide a good idea of political feasibility. Analysts could begin by identifying the policy actors who will likely play a significant role in the decision. These actors may be members of a city council or members of the National Assembly. In addition to the key formal policy actors, analysts also consider other players, such as representatives of major interest groups and administrative officials.

For each of the major policy actors, analysts try to determine their positions on the issues. One way to do this is perhaps by investigating their previous positions and decisions. Sometimes, it is possible to estimate positions based on their party membership, general political attitudes, and previous and current positions on issues that are related or similar. Their interest in the particular decision as well as the intensity of their views can be estimated or judged. These factors are likely to be shaped by the level of interest and preferences of the constituencies they represent. This will also be influenced by how much the media cover the controversy and how the issues are presented. All of this information can be pulled together to estimate political feasibility.

Analysts must remember that different actors have a different impact on feasibility. Relatively small groups with intensely held views on a subject are often capable of defeating proposals that otherwise enjoy broad support among political actors. For a great many public policy disputes, especially those that do not rise to the highest levels of visibility, political feasibility is likely to depend on the views of a small number of people and organizations.

[Figure 10-6] Protest against Importing US Beef

Factors such as public opposition need to be considered as part of political feasibility analysis.

41 Ethical Analysis

There are many situations that require extra scrutiny. Even if something is cost-effective and feasible, it does not necessarily follow that it should be done. Legal policies are not always right. Every possible policy action needs to be scrutinized for its consistency with national values. Many actions that are normal in the course of American political campaigns are seen as unethical and corrupt (if not illegal) in the Korean case.

The way the public will view an issue is a key to consistency with national ethics. The attempt to impeach President Noh

Moohyun was seen by the public as an attempt by the conservative National Assembly to overturn the results of a democratic election and the public responded by giving pro-government candidates a big victory in the following National Assembly elections.

Policy needs to be judged in terms of fairness. Is the policy based on the truth? Will it build goodwill between the people affected by the policy? Are the benefits and costs fairly distributed?

Ethical questions are not simple matters. The American philosopher John Rawls, in his *Theory of Justice* suggests one standard that a decision is just if a decision maker would make the policy not knowing whether he or she would be affected by it. The Golden Rule of treating others the way you would want to be treated is another common standard that similarly results in ethical behavior. The decision maker merely asks whether he or she would like to be treated the way their policy would treat its objects.

Ethical questions need to consider both process and outcomes. Policy analysts should be confident that their process is fair, and that the likely results are fair before accepting an alternative on ethical grounds.

The hard cases, or ethical dilemmas, involve the balancing of competing ethical claims. Is racial or ethnic profiling unacceptable in a free society that values diversity? The US federal government initially chose a system of random checks without profiling in the wake of the so-called 9-11 terrorist attacks. Many security experts complained that such a system had little chance of preventing hijacking, while it imposed high costs and inconvenience on travelers. What is the most acceptable way to promote airline security? Does profiling travelers violate their civil liberties? Even if it did, is this practice a justifiable use of government authority to protect the country? Another example is the fingerprinting requirement for many visas. The argument here, too, is that it makes travel much safer and reduces criminal traffic across borders, but it is inconvenient and reduces privacy.

[Figure 10-7] A Criminal under Arrest

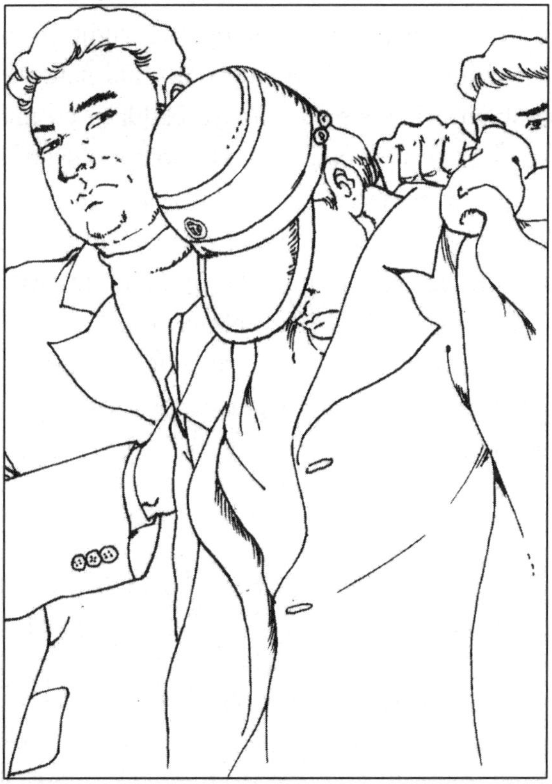

The law is a minimal standard of ethical behavior. Although not all unethical behavior is criminal, illegal behavior is almost always unethical.

Foreign workers are demanded to do work at low wages and under conditions that Koreans refuse to do, but they are subjected to very short-term limits on their work visas. They suffer from lack of familiarity with the language and culture, but must usually leave the country by the time they become comfortable and knowledgeable about Korea, its language, and culture. There is a competing value between the need for foreign workers and the need to treat them fairly and the distrust of foreigners and the desire for an ethnically-unified nation.

A recent moral dilemma involves the right to privacy in balance with child safety. Advocates of child safety insist that information about criminals who abuse children be made widely available so that people can protect their children. However, this allows no possibility for the criminal to reform their behavior. They continue to be punished forever once their name and reputation is destroyed in public by being known as a child predator. What is to be done about the falsely accused? Someone may look similar to a criminal, have committed no offense, but be subjected to a permanent loss of good name forever due to a mistake.

[Box 10-3] ***Donation Ethics***

What is the social responsibility of business? The banking sector is one of the stingiest industries in terms of spending on social contributions, according to industry data reported by the *Korea Herald* July 1, 2008.

The top eight lenders in Korea earned more than ₩10 trillion in combined profit in 2007, but their spending on charity was only ₩120 billion, or 1.2% percent of total profit as opposed to an average 2.6% for all large companies.

The banks' charitable contributions actually shrank to ₩125.1 billion from ₩126.6 billion during the same period, even as their profits increased.

The foreign banks KEB, SC First, and Citibank Korea were the stingiest.

KEB allocated a meager 0.29%, the smallest both in quantity and proportion.

Critics say that most social contributions made by local banks are aimed at marketing and promotion rather than helping the needy, with 27% of the charitable spending by the six major banks in the first half of this year going to cultural, arts, and sporting events and activities. Financial support to local communities and public service only accounted for 10% of the total contribution.

However, officials of foreign banks say that it is not fair to measure a bank's concern for social welfare by looking only at the amount of money they donate. Officials at foreign banks say that voluntary efforts by employees, including teaching practical math and economic skills directly to poor youth are not included in their total, even though their efforts are significant.

Discussion Questions

- What is the social responsibility of business?
- Foreign-owned banks may be following a different ethical culture where voluntarism is considered a more significant form of contributing to society. Should they be given credit for those efforts or are they just trying to make excuses for being cheap?
- What is the appropriate level of business donations to charity?
- What sorts of charities should they emphasize?

– Korea Herald

Discussion Questions

1. Compare some real examples that produce comparable risk with different levels of probability and consequences.
2. What are the best ways to reduce risks?
3. How can decision analysis be used in the public and private sector?
4. Write a decision tree for a real-life decision that you face. Make sure to assign probabilities.
5. Why is it important to address the future in policy analysis?
6. How is political feasibility different from other criteria? Give a real-world example.
7. What ethical standards should the government use to evaluate policy decisions? Are they different from the ones business and citizens should use?

Vocabulary

acceptability
risk assessment
severity
probability
decision analysis
decision tree
flow chart
decision node
chance node
payoff
technological risk
workplace safety
food safety
national security risk
probability of harm
severity of harm
risk management
mathematical modeling
computer modeling
computer projection
condition of uncertainty
forecast
projection
prediction
conjecture
parallel
analogy
compound interest

impact assessment
predictable impact
political feasibility analysis
contingency
party affiliation
ethical analysis
regime values
philosophical values
moral values
fairness
ethical behavior
ethical question

References

"Banks Earn Much, but Donate Little" http://www.koreaherald.co.kr/NEWKHSITE/data/html_dir/2008/07/01/200807010031.asp

Bartlett, Robert, ed. (1989). *Policy Through Impact Assessment: Institutionalized Analysis as a Policy Strategy.* Greenwood Press: New York, NY.

Behn, Robert D., and Vaupel, James W. (1982). *Quick Analysis for Busy Decision Makers.* Basic Books: New York, NY.

Bickers, Kenneth, and Williams, John (2001). *Public Policy Analysis.* Houghton Mifflin: New York, NY.

Dunn, N. William (1994). *Public Policy Analysis: An Introduction,* Prentice-Hall: Englewood Cliffs, NJ.

Huber, Peter (1999). *Hard Green: Saving the Environment from the Environmentalists* (*A Conservative Manifesto*). Basic Books: New York, NY.

"Korean Economy Mired in Stagflation" http://www.koreaherald.co.kr/NEWKHSITE/data/html_dir/2008/07/02/200807020038.asp

"Korea Ranks Among Worst in Traffic Fatality Rate" http://english.chosun.com/w21data/html/news/200806/200806040024.html

Kraft, E. Michael, and Furlong, R. Scott (2004). *Public Policy: Politics, Analysis, and Alternatives.* CQ Press: Washington, DC.

Patton, Carl V., and Sawicki, David S. (1993) *Basic Methods of Policy Analysis and Planning,* 2nd ed. Prentice Hall: Englewood Cliffs, NJ.

Presidential/Congressional Commission on Risk Assessment and Risk Management (1997). *Risk Assessment and Risk Management in Regulatory Decisionmaking.* Vol. 2: Final Report, Washington. DC: Commission on Risk Assessment and Risk Management. http://www. riskworld.com

Rawls, John (1999). *A Theory of Justice,* Revised Edition. Clarendon Press: New York, NY.

Starling, Grover (1988). *Strategies for Policy Making.* Dorsey Press: Chicago, IL.

Tong, Rosemarie (1986). *Ethics in Policy Analysis.* Prentice Hall: Englewood Cliffs, NJ.

Vedung, Evert (2005). *Public Policy and Program Evaluation.* Transaction Publishers: Piscataway, NJ.

WEEK 11 Evaluation

Summary

Evaluation is the measurement of the desirable and undesirable consequences of policies. Evaluation may focus on the process or it may look towards the outcome.

The process involves clarifying goals, setting criteria, making a model, formulating an appropriate research design, measuring the policy effects, gathering data, and analyzing and interpreting data.

The functions of evaluation include information, revealing goals, clarifying values, creating alternative policy sources, and contributing to other policy analyses.

Evaluation is concerned with government interventions, focuses on administrative outputs and outcomes, is retrospective, assesses both ongoing and finished activities, is careful, and covers more than impact assessment.

Effectiveness models may be comprehensive, evaluate goal attainment, client perspectives, or the view of stakeholders. Economic models may consider productivity or efficiency. The professional model is known as peer review.

Evaluation must address eight problems. They are the

purpose of the evaluation, who will be the evaluator and how it will be organized, how the policy will be described, how implementation is compared with the plan, what the results are, what explains the results, what the criteria are, and how the evaluation will be used.

42 Definition and Models of Policy Evaluation

Definition

Evaluation is the measurement of the desirable and undesirable consequences of a government intervention that has been taken in order to forward some policy goal. It may also relate to the procedures of fact finding about the results of government intervention and policy action.

Evaluation is a measurement of the effectiveness of the program where effectiveness should be measured in terms of the fulfillment of program's objective. It is a process which enables the administrator to describe the effects of a program and thereby to make progressive adjustments in order to reach the program goals more effectively.

Evaluation is the process of determining the merit, worth, and value of things. It is the process of distinguishing the worthwhile from the worthless, the precious from the useless.

According to Vedung, evaluation is a careful retrospective assessment of the merit, worth, and value of administration, output, and outcome of government interventions, which is intended to play a role in future, practical action situations.

Evaluation:

- Concerns government interventions
- Is focused on administration outputs and outcomes
- Is retrospective
- Assesses both ongoing and finished activities
- Is more than impact assessment
- Is a careful assessment

It is used for the purposes of:

- discovering whether objectives are being fulfilled
- finding out how well goals are being met
- determining the reasons for specific successes and failures
- uncovering the principles underlying a successful program
- increasing effectiveness
- opening the way for future research into the success of various alternatives
- redefining the means to be used for attaining objectives

Evaluation Models

Evaluation may be divided between three broad groups of models, which specify the purpose of the evaluation. These are effectiveness, economy, or professionalism. The effectiveness model, being the broadest area of concern, has four general approaches that may be further subdivided. For our purposes, effectiveness includes goal attainment evaluation, comprehensive evaluation, the client model, and the stakeholder approach. Economic models may emphasize either productivity or efficiency. The professional model is peer review.

Effectiveness Models: Goal Attainment Evaluation

Goal attainment evaluation is an effectiveness model because it asks questions about the content, output, and outcomes of the program, not about program procedures like equity or due process. It simply asks whether or not a goal has been achieved. It differs from economic and institutional models in that it only raises substantive issues. However, it does not consider program costs or the organization of the evaluation.

[Figure 11-1] Models of Evaluation

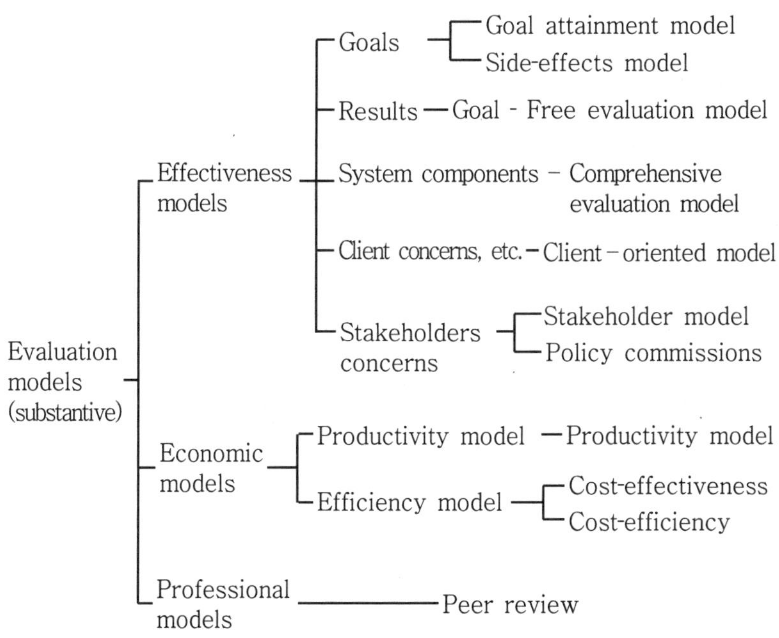

Effectiveness Models: Comprehensive Evaluation

Comprehensive evaluation models are rooted in the conviction that evaluation should be more extensive than in the narrow goal-attainment model. The process of passing judgments should not be limited to results but should at least include implementation as well as possibly including planning. In comprehensive evaluation the first task of the evaluator is to contrast the original intention with the reality and the goals with the actual outcomes.

Effectiveness Models: Client-oriented Model

Client-oriented evaluation takes the goals, expectations, concerns, or even needs of the program as seen from the point of view of the clients. At the heart of client-oriented evaluation is the question of whether the program satisfies client concerns, desires, or expectations.

Effectiveness Models: The Stakeholder Approach

The stakeholder model views the concerns and issues of the people who have an interest in or are affected by the policy intervention. Stakeholder-based evaluation starts by determining the major groups who are involved or have an interest in the emergence, execution, and results of the program. The evaluator identifies the people who created the program, who initiated and funded it, and particularly those who are charged with its implementation.

Economic Models: Productivity

Productivity can be expressed through the simple formula:

$$\text{Productivity} = \frac{\text{output}}{\text{input}}$$

Productivity as a public sector measure carries some technical advantages. Costs are not usually very difficult to calculate since agencies have calculable budgets and funds from specific sources. However, at other times it may be hard to trace specific costs because specific funds allocated and spent are often indicated as lump sums on financial reports. Outputs, on the other hand, may be exacting to catch and compute. This is even true despite that the definition of productivity includes any outputs. They are hard to compute even when they are not converted into monetary terms.

Economic Models: Efficiency

Efficiency can be measured in two ways, as cost-benefit or as cost-effectiveness. Efficiency assessments provide a frame of reference for relating costs to program results. In cost-benefit analyses, both program inputs and outcomes are measured in monetary terms. In cost-effectiveness analysis, inputs are estimated in monetary terms and outcomes in terms of actual impact.

[Figure 11-2] Efficiency as Cost-Benefit and Cost-Effectiveness

$$\text{Efficiency (cost-benefit)} = \frac{\text{Value of program effects (in KRW, US\$, etc.)}}{\text{costs (in KRW, US\$, etc.)}}$$

$$\text{Efficiency (cost-effectiveness)} = \frac{\text{program effects in physical terms}}{\text{costs (in KRW, US\$ etc.)}}$$

Professional Models: Peer Review

Peer review is mostly a screening procedure for the selection of contributions to scientific journals. Submitted articles are subjected to review by peers to decide whether they ought to be accepted for publication. Peer review is also used to offer guidance to research foundations concerning which projects should get funding. Research proposals are submitted to a group of respected colleagues for screening. On top of that, peer review has also been used to investigate and judge alleged ethical violations as well as deviations from inherited research practices. This model is constantly used in research evaluation.

Beyond the various models of evaluation, it is possible to divide each model into roughly two types. These are process evaluation, also known as formative evaluation, and outcome (or summative) evaluation.

As the names imply, process evaluation is concerned with the process of the program, how it is formed, and how it works. This form of evaluation is analogous to procedural equity in that it addresses the procedures, but is not concerned with outcomes.

Outcome evaluation (analogous to outcomes equity) is just the opposite. It is not primarily concerned with procedures or processes, except to the extent that they contribute to results. Outcome evaluation is a kind of bottom-line evaluation that looks to the end products of evaluation rather than to means or method.

Program evaluation focuses more on policy results or outcomes than on the process of implementation. Analysts use a number of methods to identify a program's goals and objectives, measure them, gather data on what program is doing, and reach some conclusions about the extents of its success. As with other policy analyses, the intent is to complete those tasks in a systematic way that fosters confidence in the accuracy of the results.

43 The Eight Problem Approach to Evaluation

There are eight primary problems of evaluation. They can be phrased as eight questions. They are:

- The purpose problem: What is the overall purpose of the evaluation?
- The organization (evaluator) problem: Who should do the evaluation and how should it be organized?
- The intervention analysis problem: How is the government intervention being evaluated, normally a policy, a program, the components of policies and programs, or the provision of services and goods, to be characterized and described? Is it regarded as a means or as a self-contained entity?
- The conversion problem: How does execution take place between the beginning of the intervention and the final outcomes?
- The results problem: What are the outputs and the outcomes – immediate, intermediate, and ultimate – of the

intervention?

- The impact problem: What contingencies (causal factors, operating casual forces)-the intervention included-explain the results?
- The criterion problem: By what value criteria should the merits of the intervention be assessed? By what standards of performance on the value criteria can success or failure or satisfactory performance be judged? What are the actual merits of the intervention?
- The utilization problem: How is the evaluation to be utilized? How is it actually used?

There is no single design or technique suitable for every program evaluation. The selection of appropriate designs and techniques depends upon the accepted definition of evaluation, the purposes of the evaluator, the question or questions to be answered, and the intended uses of the results. In other words, the evaluation depends to a great extent on the answers given for the eight problems above.

44 The Evaluation Process

The evaluation process involves six steps. In many ways it is similar to the policy development process, but it has some key differences. The six steps of evaluation are the clarification of goals, setting criteria, making a causal model, developing an appropriate research design, measurement, gathering data, and the analysis and interpretation of data.

The discussion below elaborates on the meaning and concerns of each of the various steps of evaluation.

Clarification of Goals

This step begins by determining the purpose of the evaluation. In part, this means looking at the needs of the decision makers who will be using the evaluation. In order to determine a decision maker's needs, the first question is how the decision maker perceives the program. It makes a difference if the decision maker is dissatisfied with the effectiveness or the results of the program (or with the lack of a program).

Questions include:

- Has the program met its particular social mission?
- How will the information brought out by a program evaluation be used?
- When is the final report needed?

This stage determines whether the report will focus on the short term, medium term, or long term in assessing the results of the program. Short term results need to rely more heavily on outputs as there are likely to be fewer outcomes that are measurable. The long term can capture outcomes more clearly, but they must be carefully discriminated from non-program effects.

If a job training program is evaluated for short-term results, then graduation rates from the program would be a good output measure. Outcomes in the form of job placement would be measurable in the short to medium term. At the long term, employment would have to be judged as due to the effects of the program or other factors. If there is a booming economy and there is almost no unemployment, it is hard to say what impact the job training program had.

Regardless of the decisions made about the time frame of the evaluation, any clarification of goals should include discussions with policy makers and program managers. These are exactly the target group of decision makers whose opinion can tell us how insiders perceive a program. Even if the ultimate purpose of an evaluation is to influence public opinion, it is important to know how those involved in the program see it. Discrepancies between how a program is seen by the public and by those who designed it can provide useful information that will help guide the evaluation.

Imagine the job training program. The public is disappointed because there is still unemployment. They believed the program would solve unemployment. Discussions with program managers and policy makers might determine that the program was never designed to eliminate unemployment. Its goal was to make a small group of hard-to-employ workers find better jobs. It is even possible that the program managers view it as a major success in spite of the public perception of failure.

Setting Criteria

This stage is much like the criteria stage in policy analysis. Here the concern is how to judge policy success or failure. What are the criteria that are to be used to make that judgment?

One possibility is political significance. Ultimately this means nothing more than the judgment of the evaluator that the program or policy has or has not done enough to accomplish its goals or objectives. In this case, though, the analyst will not rely on informed conjecture alone. The evaluator will gather pertinent information. This may include public, policy maker, and manager perception of the program. It may include the perception of the target population. There may be data available that suggests success or failure. The analyst should try to gather as much quantitative and qualitative data as possible to make a judgment.

Evaluative claims depend as much on facts as they do on values. To claim that a particular policy or program has attained any level of performance requires not only that policy outcomes are valuable to some individual, group, or society as a whole. It also requires that policy outcomes are actually a consequence of actions undertaken to resolve a particular problem. Therefore monitoring is a prerequisite for evaluation.

The other possibility is a statistical analysis of some sort of outcome measure, comparing it against the goal. This is a measure of statistical significance. As in statistical measures, this comes down to a measure of the percentage confidence that a result is correct. A 95% confidence level means that there is a 95% chance that it is true. Statistical significance at the 5% level means the same thing.

Social scientists and other analysts usually look for a degree of significance in excess of the 95% level. Many studies only accept results at the 99% or greater level.

Statistical theory comes with the concept of error. While there may be a 99% chance that the result is true, there is still a 1% chance that it is in error. When looking at statistical evaluations of program effect, there are four possible results:

- The evaluation says there was no effect and the program really had no effect.
- The evaluation says there was no effect but there really was one. This is referred to as "Type One Error." The

chance of type one error is measured through the calculation of the coefficient alpha. A larger alpha means a greater chance of type one error.

- The evaluation says there was an effect but there really was no effect. This is referred to as "Type Two Error." The chance of a type two error is measured through the calculation of the coefficient beta. A larger beta means a greater chance of a type two error.
- The evaluation says there was an effect and the program really had an effect.

The first and fourth cases obviously present no problem, but the evaluator must be alert for the possibility of the second and third cases.

Making a Causal Model

A model is a simplification of the real world for any purpose. Models are used widely in forecasting and many computer and board games are models that represent real events in a simplified form.

The analyst pulls together several elements in order to construct a causal model. This causal model includes a hypothesis about the cause or causes of the problem, the various variables that may be involved in the problem, and the relationships between the variables.

The dependent variable is the variable that the policy wants to change through the program intervention. Independent variables are the ones that the program directly alters, as well as other variables that may affect the dependent variable.

In a case where the policy is designed to reduce traffic

accidents caused by cell phones, the dependent variable would be the number of such accidents. The independent variables would include the policy intervention (such as a level of sanction like a fine), as well as other possible factors that might effect the accident rate. These might include the number of cell phone users, the level of any publicity campaigns about the issue, and the overall number of accidents.

The evaluator predicts the relationships between the variables. For example, as the fine increases, the number of accidents decreases. As the number of cell phone users increases, the number of accidents would increase. As the publicity increases, accidents would decrease. As the overall number of accidents increases, the number of cell phone-related accidents would also increase.

Finally, this would be stated as a hypothesis or a series of hypotheses that could test these relationships using actual data. A hypothesis is an explanation for a problem that can be tested by further investigation. Hypotheses and hypothesis testing are at the heart of the scientific process. Their usage conveys a powerful systematic procedure of scientific validation to the evaluator.

The model may be quantitative or statistical and may be expressed mathematically:

Independent variable = constant + variable 1 + variable 2...

Such a mathematical model allows for sophisticated statistical and computer analysis.

Developing an Appropriate Research Design

Evaluation is a technique of managing public organizations in which systematic data gathering and other research-like operations are important. From this perspective, evaluation using research differs from other social research mainly in regard to the problems to be addressed. It does not differ according to research designs and data-collection methods that are used. Problems, not designs or methods, provide identity to evaluation.

As such, evaluation may employ experimental, quasi-experimental, and non-experimental methods

The experimental design is the basis for scientific experiments. The classic controlled experiment includes a pre-test/post-test and a control group.

The controlled experiment selects two sub-samples at random from the sample population. The evaluator measures selected characteristics of both groups. Then one group is exposed to the program being evaluated. The evaluator then measures the selected characteristics of both populations.

The effect of exposure to the program or treatment is determined by comparing any changes in those exposed (known as the experimental group) with changes in those not exposed (known as the control group). This design can be diagrammed as in Figure 11-3.

The effect of the program is considered to be the difference between any changes that occur in the experimental group ($O_2 - O_1$) and any that occur in the control group ($O_4 - O_3$). The total effect of the program is represented by the changes in the experimental group which did not appear in the control group. This formula is, therefore, $(O_2 - O_1) - (O_4 - O_3)$.

This design is rigorous and elegant when used to determine the overall effects of a program (e.g., treatment) because it controls for any change that might occur in the experimental group other than that produced by the program or treatment. The experimental design is also appropriate for assessing effects of program strategies, techniques, and treatment if they can be isolated from others used in the program.

[Figure 11-3] Experimental Design

		Measure-ments Before	Exposure to Program	Measure-ments After
Random Assign ment	Experi-mental Group	O_1	X	O_2
	Control Group	O_3		O_4

"O" represents an observation and "X" represents the program intervention.

An experimental design is usually the preferred standard, but sometimes it is not possible to have all of the experimental elements (pre-test, post-test, and control group). The essential element that makes a design experimental is random assign-ment. Designs that otherwise look like experimental designs but lack random assignment to groups are called quasi-experimental.

If experimental design is preferred, why not have random assignment? In many real-life cases it is impossible or unethical to divide groups this way. In the case of a medicine trial, the consequences of denying treatment to one group may be too severe, for example. It is much easier to compare two non-random populations before and after an intervention. For example, a program may be implemented on a trial basis in one city, but not in another similar city. It is more difficult to determine causation in this case, but it is often the only possibility.

A third option is to gather data and analyze it statistically. This is a non-experimental design. It is relatively easy to gather data and sort out populations according to the various different measured characteristics. This makes non-experimental studies very popular, particularly in social science applications. The major limitation is that it is difficult to determine the actual reasons for variable relationships.

The choice of research design will be based on practicality and data availability. It will also be based on the purpose of the evaluation and the nature of the policy intervention.

Measurement

The task of measurement includes determining the input variables, any intervening variables, and the variable or variables representing policy results. A policy system equals:

Policy inputs + intervening variables = policy results

Of course, the evaluator wants to gather the most accurate and complete information possible. One problem that often arises in measuring the policy result is the difference between outputs and outcomes.

An output is the initial result of a policy, but it is not the goal of the program, but an intermediary result that contributes to a goal. For example, an attempt to evaluate an educational reform might measure outputs of more teachers and more school buildings. A reform of the police might have more police and more police equipment as an initial output. Generally, policy outputs are easy to measure, or at least easier to measure than outcomes.

[Figure 11-4] Evaluation May Involve Quantitative, Statistical, and Mathematical Analysis

A large part of an analyst's job is collecting and interpreting large and sophisticated sets of data.

The various policy outputs differ from policy outcomes. The policy outcomes are secondary results and represent the overall impact of a policy intervention. Outcomes better represent the goals and objectives of programs. In the education reform example, higher student test scores and other indications of better education levels would be used to measure outcomes. For the police reform example, less crime would be the preferred outcome to measure.

There are three factors to consider.

First, the target groups may differ for outputs and outcomes. Teachers and police officers are affected by outputs, whereas students and the public are affected by outcomes in the example. The evaluator should carefully consider which groups to measure.

The second consideration is that outputs are more specific, while outcomes are more general. As most goals and objectives are of a more general nature, outcomes are usually more appropriate to measure.

Finally, outputs are usually much easier to measure than outcomes. Some studies measure the number of teachers hired, schools built, police trained, equipment bought, and use that to represent success or failure. While that may be necessary in some cases, it is generally better to try to find measurable outcomes, like test scores and number of crimes to compare against goals.

Gathering Data

The process of gathering data is approached once the decisions have been made what to measure. This process is more successful when approached with creativity and imagination.

This topic is covered at greater length in Week 5, Information and Alternatives, especially sections 14~16.

Analysis and Interpretation of Data

This is the assessment of the operation. This stage includes the evaluation of the degree to which the operating program has achieved the predetermined objectives. This assessment may be scientifically done or may not. This will depend on the nature of the evaluation, and the availability of the statistical data.

On the basis of this assessment, a judgment is made as to whether the policy intervention was worthwhile. This brings us back to value formation. At this point it is possible to make value judgments. Now the evaluator may say whether the policy is successful or failed. At the end of the evaluation process, a new value may emerge, or old values may be reaffirmed, reassessed, or redefined.

45 Policy Evaluation Criteria

Much like policy analysis in general, evaluation in particular may be done on the basis of various different criteria. These criteria may include effort, efficiency, effectiveness, adequacy, equity, responsiveness, system maintenance, and process.

- Effort is a measure of what has been done. How much has been tried to achieve the goals of the program?
- Efficiency is the same as for policy analysis and is covered by the same cost/benefit measures.
- Effectiveness means the degree of policy or program goal achievement.
- Adequacy is a measure of whether enough has been done

within the scope of the program in general.

- Equity is the same as for policy analysis and in a like manner may judge the fairness of the process as well as of the outcomes of the policy intervention.
- Responsiveness measures the extent to which the needs are met of the target group or groups, as well as the needs of other stakeholders.
- System maintenance is a measure of how the policy contributes to the continued functioning of the overall political and administrative system.
- Process evaluation is a specific measure of the procedures and processes of implementing the policy intervention.

As with every other consideration in policy evaluation, the criteria selected depend on the purposes of the evaluation. An evaluation for target groups will stress responsiveness, while effort may be the desired criteria by the general public. A conservative evaluation may stress efficiency and process equity, while a liberal evaluation might look more to adequacy and outcomes equity as the chosen criteria.

Discussion Questions

1. What are the differences between the effectiveness, rational/economic, and professional models of evaluation? Which do you think is the most appropriate?
2. How should effectiveness be judged? Is it a problem when the government and the public use different models and criteria?
3. What are the problems of evaluation? How can they be solved?

4. What do you think is the most important step in the evaluation process? How should it be approached?
5. Give a real example of the difference between measuring outputs and outcomes. Explain the effect of each approach on respective evaluations of the program.

Vocabulary

policy evaluation
retroactive
effectiveness model
goal attainment evaluation
comprehensive evaluation
client oriented evaluation
stakeholder oriented evaluation
economic model
productivity
efficiency
professional model
peer review
purpose
intervention
conversion
impact
criterion
utilization
public policy dispute
level of visibility
fairness
ethical behavior
ethical question
retrospective assessment

References

Bardach, Eugene (2000). *A Practical Guide for Policy Analysis: The Eightfold Path to More Effective Problem Solving.* Chatham House: New York, NY.

Bickers, Kenneth, and Williams, John (2001). *Public Policy Analysis* Houghton Mifflin: New York, NY.

Franklin, Jack L, Thrasher, Jean H (1976). *An Introduction to Program Evaluation.* John Wiley and Sons: Toronto, Canada.

Kraft, E. Michael, and Furlong, R. Scott (2004). *Public Policy: Politics, Analysis, and Alternatives.* CQ Press: Washington, DC.

Nagel, Stuart (2002). *Handbook of Public Policy Evaluation.* Sage: Thousand Oaks, CA.

Rist, Ray C. (1995). *Policy Evaluation: Linking Theory to Practice.* Edward Elgar: Cambridge, England.

Rossi, Peter H, Freeman, Howard E (1982). *Evaluation: A Systematic Approach,* 2nd ed. Sage: Beverly Hills, CA.

Vedung, Evert (2005) *Public Policy and Program Evaluation.* Transaction Publishers: Piscataway, NJ.

WEEK 12 Student Presentations

These weeks are reserved for student projects. Students must do a group project in English. The projects are designed as group projects in order to prepare students for the collaborative nature of policy work.

Group Size

Each project must be prepared and presented in a group of three students. If there are unusual circumstances due to the size of the class, the professor may adjust the group size. However, no work should go forward until the group has received the approval of the professor.

Project Length

The project must be presented in English to the class. The presentation should last less than ten minutes, with an additional ten minutes allotted for discussion time.

Paper Submission

A written version of the entire project should be submitted to the professor after revisions. The written version should match the contents of the oral presentation and should be less than 20 pages in length.

Topics

Groups can choose any single public policy for analysis. The group should agree on the topic and get the professor's approval before they begin research. Policies may be chosen from any general policy area. Policy areas that may be addressed include economic policy, social welfare policy, environmental policy, trade policy, education policy, health policy, foreign policy, cultural policy, tourism, industrial policy, defense policy, construction policy, law enforcement policy, and any other policy area that is approved by the professor.

Contents

The presentation and paper should include the following information:

- What the issue is
- How the issue entered the public agenda
- What the goal is
- How the goal is achieved
- Who the actors are
- Who wins and loses

Presenting in English

Remember the audience. No speech can be one-size-fits-all. Make sure to set clear objectives at the start to orient the audience and prepare them what to expect. Try to respond to the audience's expectations and tailor your content to the audience by presenting the information they need to know. Finally, make the presentation interesting and get the audience involved.

Organize your information. Make a clear structure that you readily understand and can remember. Design your introduction and conclusion for the greatest impact. Practice delivering your message within the allowed time. Share your structure with the audience to help forge links with the audience.

Use visuals effectively. Design them to present information that highlights aspects of your presentation for maximum impact. Practice handling visuals to use them smoothly. Choose a clear and simple format to highlight important information. Give handouts if necessary.

Use body language. Be relaxed, positive, positive, and confident to help relax the audience and set them at ease. Use eye contact to engage the audience. Use limited body movement to focus attention and highlight meaning, but avoid distracting mannerisms that take away from your message.

Deliver your message effectively. Pace yourself carefully. Adjust your language to fit the audience. Be prepared to slow down and use easier vocabulary to present to an audience with more limited comprehension. Remember that your audience is made up of students like you, so prepare a presentation that you would want to listen to.

Prepare thoroughly. Practice and refer to brief notes during the presentation. Do not plan to read your presentation.

Introduction

Introduce the title and subject of your presentation or your section of the presentation. Highlight the main points of your talk. Acknowledge the audience, and try to form a human bond with them by identifying with their situation (I know you have a lot to listen to a lot of talks today, so I will try to keep this brief). Then transition to the actual message of the speech.

The Body

The body should include all of the contents required for the presentation. Each student should present his or her part in turn. Students should use parallel language in a parallel structure to refer to the topics and points of the presentation. Repetition of key concepts is okay as the audience has no written work in front of them for reference.

Do not mindlessly repeat the same information over and over, however.

The Conclusion

The closing repeats and reviews the main points of the presentation, as well as the supporting arguments of the body.

Transitions between Students

Practice the speech beforehand to make sure that it fits in the allotted time. Make sure that each student knows where to be at every time and that the next student is ready to go when the current speaker is finished.

If you are using PowerPoint or some other visuals, the student who is using the visual should not be the next speaker. With three students, one should be speaking, one should be ready to speak, and one should be handling the visuals.

Rules

Finally, here are some basic rules of presentation.

Be Clear

You have done a lot of research and know a lot about your

topic. The audience does not. Make your subject as clear as possible. Define terms, and repeat where possible.

Be Organized

Have an outline and a plan. Practice the presentation in advance. Know what you will do when something goes wrong. Be ready to ask for help and know what sort of help you will need.

Keep track of time. Prepare less than you think you will need to fill your time, but be ready to for it to go over time and have a plan for how to cut things down to time. In addition, make sure that you have materials to add detail if your presentation ends up being too short.

Be Interesting

Remember your audience. The best way to keep their attention is by doing things to pull them in. an unusual approach, visuals, activities, questions to the audience, and an attempt to be entertaining will help engage the audience.

Be Positive

A positive and optimistic attitude is a huge determiner of success. If you believe in yourself, you are more likely to succeed. If you are positive, your audience will be more likely to respond in kind, encouraging you with positive feedback.

Negativity teaches you that you will not succeed and pulls you back. Why chose to fail when it is hard enough to succeed?

Do Not Read

Reading is about the easiest way to kill a good presentation. Reading discourages clarity (unless you are trained to read for an audience). Reading is harder to organize as you cannot add or drop material very easily. You cannot pay attention to the audience and their needs while reading. You cannot pay attention to the time while reading. Reading is not very interesting for the listener. It is difficult to project a positive attitude while you are reading. Reading is often an indication that you have a negative attitude and do not trust yourself.

Do Not Go For Too Long

No one ever complains that a speech is too short. When you go a minute over, the audience will start to dislike a good speech. One of the easiest things you can do to gain audience appreciation is by keeping good time. Going on for too long is extremely selfish and inconsiderate of the needs of others.

Bibliography

Amy, Douglas J. (1984). "Why Policy Analysis and Ethics are Incompatible." *Journal of Policy analysis and Management* 3: 573-591.

Anderson, Charles W. (1979). "The Place of Principles in Policy Analysis." *American Political Science Review* 73: 711-723.

Anderson, James E. (2003). *Public Policymaking*, 5th ed. Houghton Mifflin: Boston, MA.

Bardach, Eugene (2000). *A Practical Guide for Policy Analysis: The Eightfold Path to More Effective Problem Solving.* Chatham House: New York, NY.

Bartlett, Robert, ed. (1989). *Policy Through Impact Assessment: Institutionalized Analysis as a Policy Strategy.* Greenwood Press: New York, NY.

Bickers, Kenneth, and Williams, John (2001). *Public Policy Analysis.* Houghton Mifflin: New York, NY.

Birkland, A. Thomas (2001). *An Introduction to the Policy Process: Theories, Concepts, and Models of Public Policy Making.* M.E. Sharpe: Armonk, NY.

Behn, Robert D., and Vaupel, James W (1982). *Quick Analysis for Busy Decision Makers* Basic Books: New York, NY.

Bovbjerg, Randall R. (1985). "What Is Policy Analysis?." *Journal of Policy Analysis and Management,* 5 (1), Autumn: 154-158.

Carver, Robert H. (1996). "Where Does Policy Analysis Belong in the Undergraduate Public Administration Major?" *PS: Political Science and Politics,* 29 (3), Sept.: 521-525.

deLeon, Peter (1997). *Democracy and the Policy Sciences.* State

University of New York Press: Albany, NY.

"Do Candlelight Protests Hint at Anti-American Sentiments?" http://english.hani.co.kr/arti/english_edition/e_national/295066.html

"Don't Railroad Changes to English Teaching Through" http://english.chosun.com/w21data/html/news/200802/200802140012.html

Dunn, N. William (1994). *Public Policy Analysis: An Introduction.* Prentice-Hall: Englewood Cliffs, NJ.

"Exposing Ex-Minister's Deception Is Child's Play" http://english.chosun.com/w21data/html/news/200806/200806250028.html

"Fighting the Future with the Rhetoric of Yesteryear" http://english.chosun.com/w21data/html/news/200607/200607310036.html

Franklin, Jack L, Thrasher, Jean H (1976). *An Introduction to Program Evaluation.* John Wiley and Sons: Toronto, Canada.

Freeman, A. Myrick III (2000). "Economics, Incentives, and Environmental Regulation" in *Environmental Policy,* 4th ed. Edited by Norman J. Vig and Michael E. Kraft. CQ Press: Washington, DC.

"Gender Wage Gap Biggest in OECD." http://www.koreaherald.co.kr/NEWKHSITE/data/html_dir/2008/07/01/200807010059.asp

Goldenburg, Jacob, Mazursky, David, and Solomon, Sorin (1999). "Creative Sparks." *Science,* September 3:1495-1496

Henry, Nicholas (1992). *Public Administration and Public Affairs,* 5th ed. Prentice-Hall: Englewood Cliffs, NJ.

"High Oil Prices Forcing Truck Drivers out of Business" http://english.hani.co.kr/arti/english_edition/e_national/289886.html

Huber, Peter (1999). *Hard Green: Saving the Environment from the Environmentalists* (*A Conservative Manifesto*). Basic Books: New York, NY.

Kingdon, John W. (1995). *Agendas, Alternatives, and Public Policies,* 2nd ed. Harper Collins College: New York, NY.

"Koreans in U.S. not Scared of Beef" http://www.koreaherald.co.kr/NEWKHSITE/data/html_dir/2008/07/01/200807010030.asp

"Korean Language Proficiency Drops"

http://english.chosun.com/w21data/html/news/200807/20080703001 9.html

"Korean Economy Mired in Stagflation"
http://www.koreaherald.co.kr/NEWKHSITE/data/html_dir/2008/07/0 2/200807020038.asp

"Koreans Pay Highest Prices for Daily Necessities"
http://english.chosun.com/w21data/html/news/200807/20080702000 9.html

"Korea Ranks Among Worst in Traffic Fatality Rate"
http://english.chosun.com/w21data/html/news/200806/200806040 024.html

"Korea, U.S. Close to Beef Agreement"
http://english.chosun.com/w21data/html/news/200804/200804170 015.html

"Korea, U.S. Compromise on Farm Goods, Textiles"
http://english.chosun.com/w21data/html/news/200609/200609080 023.html

Kraft, Michael E. (2000). "Policy Design and the Acceptability of Environmental Risks: Nuclear Waste Disposal in Canada and the United States." *Policy Studies Journal,* 28 (1): 206-218.

Kraft, Michael E., and Furlong, R. Scott (2004). *Public Policy: Politics, Analysis, and Alternatives.* CQ Press: Washington, DC.

Lindblom, Charles E., and Woodhouse, Edward J. (1993). *The Policy-Making Process.* 3rd ed. Prentice Hall: Upper Saddle River, NJ.

Lynn, Laurence E. Jr. (1999). A Place at the Table: Policy Analysis, Its Postpositive Critics, and the Future of Practice. *Journal of Policy Analysis and Management,* 18 (3). (Summer): 411-425.

MacRae, Duncan, Whittington, Dale (1997). *Expert Advice for Policy Choice.* Georgetown University Press: Washington, DC.

MacRae, Duncan, Wilde, James A (1979). *Policy Analysis for Public Decisions.* Druxbury: North Scituate, MA.

Mazmanian, Daniel A., and Kraft, Michael A. (1999). *Toward Sustainable Communities: Transition and Transformations in Environmental Policy.* MIT Press: Cambridge, MA.

Miringhoff, Marc, and Miringhoff, Marque-Luisa (1999). *Social Health of the Nation: How America is Really Doing.* Oxford: New York, NY.

Nagel, Stuart (2002). *Handbook of Public Policy Evaluation.* Sage: Thousand Oaks, CA.

"New Beef Agreement Still Leaves Room for Mad Cow Fears" http://english.hani.co.kr/arti/english_edition/e_national/294857.html

"N. Koreans Fare No Worse on TOEFL Than S.Koreans" http://english.chosun.com/w21data/html/news/200802/200802150018.html

Patton, Carl V., and Sawicki, David S. (1993). *Basic Methods of Policy Analysis and Planning,* 2nd ed. Prentice Hall: Englewood Cliffs, NJ.

Poister, H. Theodore (1984). *Public Program Analysis: Applied Research Methods.* University Park Press: Baltimore, MD.

Presidential/Congressional Commission on Risk Assessment and Risk Management (1997). *Risk Assessment and Risk Management in Regulatory Decisionmaking,* Vol. 2: Final Report, Washington, DC: Commission on Risk Assessment and Risk Management. http://www. riskworld.com

"The Prosecution's Role as the Government's Strong Arm" http://english.hani.co.kr/arti/english_edition/e_editorial/295927.html

"Public Companies to be Made Private" http://english.hani.co.kr/arti/english_edition/e_business/289354.html

Rawls, John (1999). *A Theory of Justice,* Revised Edition. Clarendon Press: New York, NY.

Rein, Martin (1976). *Social Science and Public Policy.*: Penguin Books: New York, NY.

Rist, Ray C. (1995). *Policy Evaluation: Linking Theory to Practice.* Edward Elgar: Cambridge, England.

Rossi, Peter H, Freeman, Howard E. (1982). *Evaluation: A Systematic Approach,* 2nd ed. Sage: Beverly Hills, CA.

Sabatier, Paul A., ed. (1999). *Theories of the Policy Process.* Westview Press: Boulder, CO.

Sabatier, Paul A., Jenkins-Smith, Hank C., eds. (1993). *Policy*

Change and Learning: An Advocacy Coalition Approach. Westview Press: Boulder, CO.

Schneider, Anne L., and Ingram, Helen (1997). *Policy Design for Democracy.* University of Kansas Press: Lawrence, KS.

"Sex Crimes Among Korean Youth on the Rise"
http://english.chosun.com/w21data/html/news/200805/200805130024.html

Soumelis, Constantin G. (1977). *Project Evaluation: Methodologies and Techniques.* UNESCO: Paris, France.

"S. Korea's Policy on North Becoming Tougher"
http://english.hani.co.kr/arti/english_edition/e_northkorea/294560.html

Starling, Grover (1988). *Strategies for Policy Making.* Dorsey Press: Chicago, IL.

Stokey, Edith, and Zeckhauser, Richard (1978). *A Primer for Policy Analysis.* W.W. Norton & Company: New York, NY.

Stone, Deborah (2002). *Policy Paradox: The Art of Political Decisionmaking.* W.W. Norton: New York, NY.

Tong, Rosemarie (1986). *Ethics in Policy Analysis.* Prentice Hall: Englewood Cliffs, NJ.

"The Truth About 'PD Diary'"
http://english.chosun.com/w21data/html/news/200806/200806260023.html

"U.S. Base Move 'to Cost More Than W8.9 Trillion'"
http://english.chosun.com/w21dta/html/news/200806/200806090008.html

Vedung, Evert (2005). *Public Policy and Program Evaluation.* Transaction Publishers: Piscataway, NJ.

Vig, Norman J. (2003). "Presidential Leadership and the Environment" in *Environmental Policy,* 5th ed. Edited by Norman J. Vig and Michael A. Kraft. CQ Press: Washington, DC.

Weimer, L. David, and Vining, R. Aidan (2005). *Policy Analysis: Concepts and Practice*. Pearson Prentice Hall: Englewood Cliffs, NJ.

Weiss, Carol H. (1992). *Organizations for Policy Analysis: Helping Government Think.* Sage: Newbury Park, CA.

"Where's the Beef?"
http://www.thenation.com/doc/20080707/cumings

Whiteman, David (1995). *Communication in Congress: Members, Staff, and the Search for Information.* University of Kansas Press: Lawrence, KS.

Wilson, James Q. (1977). *Thinking about Crime.* Vintage Books: New York, NY.

Index

Q

R